How to Understand Marriage

Jean-Pierre Bagot

How to Understand Marriage

SCM PRESS LTD

Translated by John Bowden from the French
Pour vivre le Mariage
published 1986 by Les Editions du Cerf,
29 bd Latour-Mabourg, Paris

© Les Editions du Cerf 1986

Translation © John Bowden 1987

Nihil obstat: Father Anton Cowan
Censor

Imprimatur: Rt. Rev. John Crowley, VG
Westminster, 1 April 1987

The Nihil obstat *and* Imprimatur *are a declaration that
a book or pamphlet is considered to be free from doctrinal
or moral error. It is not implied that those who have granted
the* Nihil obstat *and* Imprimatur *agree with the contents,
opinions or statements expressed.*

British Library Cataloguing in Publication Data

Bagot, Jean-Pierre
How to understand marriage.
1. Marriage—Religious aspects—
Christianity
I. Title II. Pour vivre le mariage.
English
261.8'3581 BT706

ISBN 0–334–02040–9

First published in English 1987
by SCM Press Ltd, 26–30 Tottenham Road, London N1 4BZ
Typeset at The Spartan Press Ltd
Lymington, Hants
and printed in Great Britain by
Richard Clay Ltd, Bungay, Suffolk

Contents

Introduction

How can Christian marriage come alive? There are plenty of good books on this subject, and I do not claim to have anything new to say about it. But is that the first question to ask? Given the new difficulties which so many couples come up against nowadays, of course there will be no end of reflecting on their psychological, social and moral problems. More than ever there is a need to help families in distress; they are often plunged into a social and cultural world which gives them a severe battering. The transformation of the way in which we live deepens the hope that many young people attach to the success of a union which they see as the only possible guarantee against the loneliness and underlying anxieties of our world; but emotional disillusionment and inter-personal conflict are often only made worse by marriage – we can see this from the growing number of divorces.

These very difficulties lead people to ask a prior question. Is getting married worth the trouble? Is it worth the bother of having a Christian marriage? What is the point of a step which raises quite basic questions: 'What contribution does it make to love?' 'What difference does it make to family life?'

This specific, limited issue is the one with which I want to try to deal. At a time when the *raison d'être* of Christian marriage has been put in question, I want to make it clearer that marriage does have a meaning, that it is a pattern for expressing love in a different way, that it offers an opportunity for saving it.

I have written this book in the first place for young people in love – they may want to prepare for marriage or they may reject the idea. They may have chosen to wait for the ceremony before uniting, or they may already be living together. They may be discussing marriage with their families and friends or they may be in open conflict with them. The starting point does not matter much here. The only thing that matters is that they should be ready to reflect on their situation. What do we want? Where are we going? How can our love succeed?

I have also written it for older people, for the parents of these young couples: they are very often disturbed, sometimes made aggressive by certain types of behaviour. I shall not be saying that the young are right and the older ones are wrong, but be trying to help the latter to see what meaning can emerge out of situations which they do not always understand, and which they sometimes reject violently. I want to help them to deepen their own view of marriage, of *their* marriage, so that they can sometimes be of positive help to those are are dear to them.

Finally, I hope that this book will be of help to clergy. They are often divided and deeply uneasy. In a pastoral context they are normally led to try to understand those whose attitudes might seem ambiguous in order to give them better support. But if they do that, they are accused of accepting all and sundry, of cheapening morals and faith. They are torn between the demands of an ecclesiastical law which only recognizes as valid a union of baptized persons which has officially been contracted in the face of the church, and the need to encourage the spiritual development of young people whose faith in this church is shaky. But sometimes they lack a clear vision of what would allow them to avoid a ruinous choice between all or nothing, between moralizing disclaimers leading to a break and the vulnerable acceptance of situations which conflict with the vocation to love which it is their responsibility to hold before the world.

It is to all these people that I want to extend an invitation to read about Christian marriage, that is to say, to see what the church offers in its sacrament.

1

Marriage on Trial

Christian disarray in the face of crisis

The institution of marriage is in a state of crisis, but couples seem to be getting on better than ever. Everything suggests that in a world in which men and women feel increasingly weighed down by the constraints of all kinds which society imposes on them, they are jealously defending what seems to them to be the place of intimacy and freedom: love is standing out against the law. Why the registry office, why the church, when one is in love? Why encumber oneself with old-fashioned principles and reject divorce when love is dead?

This situation, with numerous variations, is the source of painful conflicts between generations.

The point of view of the young

The young people who provoke these conflicts are sometimes the first to be upset. A number of them, in favour of 'trial marriages' or quite simply living together, would ask no more than to continue to live in harmony with those around

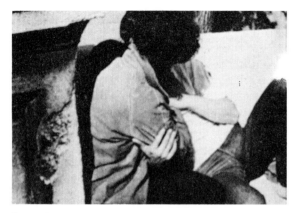

Lover's seat: ancient and modern.
Photo R. Kalvarl Magnum

them. They are saddened to see the hurt their attitude causes. But they do not want to make things worse. They want to have their day, and mean to see that they get it. Why can't other people understand their problems and see their point of view!

The parents' point of view

Parents who have been able to live an authentic Christian married life are disconcerted by what they see among their children. Is this the result of their love lived out in faith? They don't know how to react. When they welcome their children back home, do they have to accept 'illegitimate couples'? Do they give them the same room to share? That causes problems, above all when there are younger children. Are they apparently to take as 'normal' something that they cannot accept in their heart of hearts? Should they press for marriage? Christian marriage? Why don't these young people say clearly and openly that they plan to spend their lives together, if they are really serious?

The questioning is painful enough when the parents belong to circles in which 'that sort of thing isn't done'. It becomes even more so when married couples, convinced Christians, come to ask whether their past domestic life has not been ridiculously idealistic, and at any rate out of date. Even the faith which had supported their commitment before God can be put in question.

Questions raised for the church

So believers turn to the church and ask it to say something. But that sometimes only increases the difficulties. Official declarations recalling clear principles are criticized because they are idealistic or too sharp, unsuited to particular circumstances. Mature believers can certainly recognize their profound value. But what authority do they have for those who do not accept, or have come to reject, the ecclesiastical logic which considers all those who are baptized as subject to the church's rules? It is this very logic which many young people are challenging. Non-believers or semi-believers do not see why they should submit to a legislation which is imposed on them in the name of a baptism by which they do not feel committed.

But believers are just as opposed to the attitude

The old lovers. *Photo Edimedia*

of certain priests whom they would describe as lax: by agreeing to enter into dialogue with young people, are they not destroying all terms of reference? In meetings for marriage preparation, in which they seem to accept on the same footing as anyone else couples who live together, or at least who have regular sexual relations before marriage, are they not mocking those who take seriously Christian demands about sexuality? This latter group expects support from the church to justify its convictions and to reinforce its struggle to maintain Christian norms. And here are representatives of the church who seem to be betraying them!

Principles demolished

Is it then enough to recall the *principles* of Christian marriage to those whom the church can still reach, even if they are more or less remote from the church and its teaching? But what if a priest or a lay Christian responsible for marriage preparation explains to two young people the *demands* of this church in relation to the sacrament that it offers? These demands will perhaps be listened to if they represent good advice about a certain number of psychological, legal or physiological problems which young people feel that they have not yet worked out. But the sacrament itself is quite a different matter.

The fidelity and indissolubility of the married couple

This is the basic commitment that the church demands of those who come to be married in its presence.

'That is indeed my dearest wish,' says someone in love. 'May the other person become my be-all and end-all! Then what might seem to be an external constraint will become the very law of my love.'

But who can keep up such an illusion once he or she sees what in fact is going on? What young person has not witnessed the slow degradation of his or her home? How many of them have found in their own family a reason for believing that deep fidelity is possible? What beloved does not prove deceitful sooner or later? Is it conceivable that just one human being can ever respond to all the physical, emotional or even spiritual expectations of someone seeking to live a full life?

In fact marriage might seem to be a lottery in which the risk of losing is no less great than the chance of winning. To be able to promise the other complete and eternal fidelity, one partner should at least be sure of knowing who this partner is. If the church wants to maintain its demands, it should accept 'trial marriages'! That would at least make it possible to look before one leapt, to enter into a commitment on the basis of experience.

That is how realistic lovers think. They would certainly want to believe that their dream of ideal love could provide a basis for the fidelity which is called for. But once they come into contact with the bitter spectacle of everyday reality, they are led to envisage another hypothesis. They are then put off by the absolute character of what is required of them. How is it possible to make a loyal promise to remain faithful to one's spouse and never seek a divorce?

13

Fertility

The Roman Catholic church affirms that marriage leads to having children, and it refuses to recognize as valid a commitment which would *a priori* exclude children. But it goes even further: it censures as immoral any sexual practice which takes artificial steps against procreation.

Certainly we want a child, people in love will usually reply. But how can we give a child the sort of place he or she might once have had when we live in an overpopulated world and the struggle to find one's place in society has become so difficult? Moreover, children were once regarded as 'props for old age': they would take direct care of their parents when these became too old to work. That may still be true in certain countries today. But in the 'developed' world, the welfare state offers much greater security. So long live the child which gives the couple a happy balance! Down with ill-considered risks! No to interference!

That is the instinctive reaction of people in love. So how can one accept without qualification the church's commendation of large families?

Chastity

Without question the time is past when a Puritan scorn for the body led to considering sexual intercourse as a duty which deserved to be pleasurable in the act since this was aimed at propagating the species, but was otherwise always somewhat suspect. But why go on claiming to extinguish even the least spark of desire by submitting it to the 'permission of the church'? Why these prohibitions against full sexual intercourse before marriage? Why still talk of 'conjugal chastity' after marriage? Why affirm the value of a degree of physical asceticism or the need for periodic continence? What is love if it is not represented by constant embrace of and embracing by the beloved?

Those are the defences of people in love. So

In the closed world of the village, rejection is often total. *Photo J-L. Charmet*

how can they accept the validity of a morality defined by celibates living in a totally different world from their own?

Official commitment

The church asks that marriage should be contracted in conditions which give it a legitimate and public character. For baptized persons it recognizes as valid only a union contracted according to certain precise rules, and before its official representative.

But why an official contract? Is that not to look for support from false security and thus get out of recreating day by day the original sparkle of a mutual gift? Surely the constraint of a legal commitment can only kill the freedom without which love could not live! Why even have to take as witnesses third parties who are more or less strangers to the concerns of an intimate little group? Certainly the ceremony should still be celebrated in the closer circle of those whom one expects to share the joy of the couple about to come into being. But this festival must come in its own time, and above all it must avoid those 'formalities' which so destroy its spontaneity.

Those who are in love continue to make basic protests of this kind. Dreaming of an encounter which is new each day, taking as a basis the authenticity of their feelings and their desire of the moment, they rebel against the concern of society to give this desire a framework, to regulate it.

And marriage? Marriage in church? If they accept it they are often only keeping up appearances. They accept it to the degree that it prevents their cutting themselves off from dear ones and brings more sparkle to the feast of life.

A shift of values in society

One of the most disconcerting aspects of the present crisis is that it is not just a religious one. What is now in question is the very principle, which was uncontested at other times, of the legitimate family as a basic unit of society.

How are we to understand this phenomenon? Here we need sociological analysis; the world of former times is no longer today's world. Its transformation explains the change in mentality.

An economic shift

In former times, given that society was based on the principle of the family, spontaneous love, eros, only rarely had the right to express itself. What counted above all else in marriage was the guarantee that it provided of both the conservation and the perpetuation of the patrimony, not only among the upper classes of society but also in the peasant world. The choice of a husband or wife thus affected everyone's welfare. Marriage was primarily a concern for parents, to such a degree that the son and, with more reason, the daughter who went against his or her parents'

will was held to be answerable before the law. One really did have to live in destitution if one renounced any concern for dowry, hopes or rank.

Socially, at that time the greatest danger was that of the illegitimate child. Parents were obsessed with preserving their daughters' 'virtue', this virtue very often being in fact simply a guarantee for the future.

In our present-day world, that of the 'nuclear' family in which every generation lives independently of its predecessor, all this has almost ceased to count. Marriage based on family interests has certainly not disappeared completely, and probably never will. But the future of a new couple now no longer depends so much on the family patrimony (even if there is no denying the advantages which certain family situations initially bring) as on the personal experience and skills of individuals, which are based for the most part on the support of the whole of society (education, social guarantees). Generally speaking, love is no longer subject to the old imperatives. How can the marriage contract not be affected?

15

A man's view. The Kiss, Rodin. Marble, 1886. Musée Rodin, Paris. *Photo Bruno Janet*

A woman's view. Abandonment, Camille Claudel, 1905. Museé Rodin, Paris. *Photo Bruno Janet*

Sexual liberation

We live in the age of 'sexual liberation'. Modern knowledge of physiological processes allows us to control fertility. The illegitimate child is hardly a risk any more. The social basis for the prohibition against sexual life outside marriage or without the intention of marriage has collapsed. Sexual need, emotional and physical, can blossom without necessarily having to go through the institution.

Moreover, the modern psychological revolution is beginning to have its full effect. Now that they have lost their social basis, prohibitions are disappearing among most people. Those with some knowledge of psychology then have fun denouncing the 'repressions' of yesterday's world.

In reaction to a past which people no longer understand, pleasure becomes the order of the day. Everything encourages it. From now on the one at whom the finger is pointed is no longer the one who 'goes wrong' but the one who stands out from others by his or her chaste behaviour.

A social shift

The family then ceases to be the necessary and unchallengable basis of society. A woman, an unmarried mother (unmarried sometimes against her will but often quite voluntarily) or divorced people have their place in this world. It is clear that children without a father or born into broken marriages can suffer from the emotional consequences of their situation for a long time. But the damaging consequences are sufficiently far off for it to be possible to pretend to ignore the relationship between cause and effect. And if one day the consequences of the past prove too serious, people may well be content to look for palliatives for them without investigating the deeper reasons for the instability or even the delinquency. Modern society is finally accommodating itself to the new situation.

A 'political' shift

By 'political' shift I mean a transformation in our way of looking at the powers which govern the way in which society functions.

The organization of yesterday's world was like a pyramid. At the top was the chief, the king, the emperor (or the pope in the spiritual order), a direct representative of God and guarantor of world order. At the lower levels were different officials who shared in an indisputed authority depending on their own particular functions. The problem for society at that time was the perpetuation of this order. New generations were called on to follow *tradition*.

In this situation the celebration of marriage could be thought to serve the transmission of power in a certain way. A new family, based on the authority of the one who became its head, took over from the old one. Or more exactly, the old one was extended in the new one.

But from now on we live in a world in which innovation is what is called for. The phenomenon does not just apply to technology. It stamps our mentality. 'Old hat', 'out of date', these are the phrases which young people instinctively use when faced with any authoritarian statement which claims to be establishing tradition. They are equally used of the church, which is seen as being tied up with the ancient world. Calls to order from 'on high' are *a priori* regarded as suspect or devoid of interest. They can only become significant if they seem capable of verification in present experience and as a source of development for the future. So their value does not derive from the authority which proclaims them. Those who still maintain communication with the representatives of this authority no longer consider that their experience is determinative. As far as morals are concerned, the authority for decisions no longer lies in the past, it lies with young people.

This modification of the vertical relationship runs parallel to what we might call a horizontal transformation. The members of yesterday's society lived in a closed world, without communication with other forms of thought or culture than those of their own tradition. That is all finished. Through travel and modern means of communication young people discover other ways of thinking and living from those of their ancestors. Voices from the past are now mixed with those from other worlds, and are sometimes drowned. How can apparently nebulous conceptions about marriage not be affected?

A religious shift

In former days the religious institution represented the crown of the secular institution by giving it ultimate significance. It legitimated and sacralized what appeared so self-evident that it could not but be regarded as the will of God. The church and society were above discussion. Born Christians, people remained sociologically Christians.

But how could religion not be involved in the new trend? In many respects its language appears to be no more than a fossilized rite which people accept only for aesthetic or sentimental reasons, seeking to maintain a bond with past generations that they do not want to sever.

But is that necessarily the fate of the sacrament offered by the church?

Rediscovering a language

People live in this new situation without always thinking about it. And that explains the non-communication that I mentioned at the beginning.

In families this non-communication is expressed in conflicts, whether open or masked. One often finds it in the dialogue that seems to be opening up between young people who ask the church to bless their marriage and the priest who speaks in its name. Certainly the former only rarely say what they feel when confronted with someone whom they see as an administrative authority to which it is better to submit without saying anything. However, the underlying connotations are very much there.

The difficulty returns when it comes to deciding what form the service is to take. The future bride and groom may well feel tongue-tied when confronted with the passages of the Bible from which they will be asked to choose for the reading at their wedding. Apart perhaps from the magnificent love poem, the Song of Songs, these texts will seem to them to derive from a foreign world. They would like to be able to substitute their own texts, poems or songs reflecting what they really think. The language of the church and that of spontaneous love are out of phase.

So does the church have nothing to say which might have a bearing on the profound preoccupations, whether conscious or vaguely felt, of those who come to ask it to celebrate their love?

For through their objections, whether or not these are expressed, they are perceiving a disconcerting reality. Love is fragile. How is disillusionment to be avoided? Where does one find the assurance and certainty of which one dreams? Perhaps one makes a show of them, but at the same time has a feeling of not really possessing them.

Is it not necessary to rediscover a language which is other than the repetition of principles? Not that the value of principles is to be denied. But they presuppose a long journey. How can they be shown to be the crystallization of a long experience that each young couple will have to make in their turn and for themselves? How can they be shown to indicate the conditions, which are sometimes difficult, needed for love really to succeed, for its salvation?

It is by rereading what the Bible tells us with new eyes that we can reply to these questions. In that way we discover through profoundly human events the story of marriage in the people of God. For in this story we can recognize problems which are still topical. It can then allow each person truly to look at love as God intends it. By offering a way of understanding the impasses into which a degree of spontaneity can lead it reveals the way to success. In this way it can give new meaning to demands and rites which no longer seem empty shells because the kernel within them has been forgotten.

2

Marriage in the Old Testament

A history of contrasts

How should we read the biblical texts about marriage?

It is always tempting to read the biblical texts in a dogmatic way; in that case they are regarded as an expression of eternal truths which must be taken literally. And people forget that scripture brings us the story of a quest prompted by the Spirit. Summoned by the divine call, the people of God has gradually discovered the whole tenor of sayings or demands which at first were interpreted in a confused or even erroneous way.

As far as marriage is concerned, this type of reading (which is known as a fundamentalist reading) can lead to real contradictions.

By appealing to certain texts (descriptions of a given situation, legal writings) it justifies customs which the progress of revelation has subsequently caused to be revised. So it was that in the sixteenth century, at the time of the Reformation, a Protestant prince thought he could justify his bigamy by appealing to the polygamy which was long accepted among the Hebrew people. Similarly, the Mormon sect wanted to reintroduce polygamy until the civil law of the United States prohibited it.

The opposite mistake consists in gluing together systematically all the fumblings and mistakes of a particular time on the pretext of implementing the absolute value of the law. Only those biblical texts are retained which seem to us to be moral in the current perspective of the church. That is to forget that real spiritual discovery takes place along a slow and difficult road. It is also to fail to recognize that human beings have only been able to discover the real demands of love through failures and even mistakes. By contrast the Bible does not give us ready-made solutions that only have to be applied directly. It shows us a trajectory that we are called to follow in the conditions of our present-day world.

In this perspective the basic biblical statements about husband and wife do not appear as legislation coming *a priori* and from the outside to curb human enthusiasm. They present themselves as good news discovered bit by bit, after a good deal of trial and error and as a reply to a profound avowal of love. They show us what it means to be a married couple, and the significance of marriage.

Female statuette in obsidian found at Catalhöyük in Anatolia, sixth millennium. Archaeological museum of Ankara

logy which he gives of Jesus, three of the four women that he mentions, Tamar, Rahab, Ruth and Bathsheba, are victims of this violence.

Hardly brilliant moral examples

In the Old Testament there is nothing idyllic about the description of sexual and matrimonial customs. Reflection on the significance of love and marriage takes place only slowly, against a background of sexual violence and a mercantile view of 'trading in women', who are often seen as objects of erotic desire or as providers of male descendants.

Although we are accustomed to pass discreetly over these facts it is striking to see that the evangelist Matthew stresses them. In the genea-

Tamar

In the book of Genesis (38.6–30) we are told that Judah secured descendants only by an act of incest. Tamar, his daughter-in-law, had remained childless after the death of her two successive husbands, sons of Judah. She could not get her father-in-law to give her his third son, Shelah, in marriage, as was provided for by the levirate law which obliged a brother to assure descendants if his other brothers had died childless. So Tamar disguised herself as a prostitute and succeeded in seducing her father-in-law, by whom she became pregnant, thus assuring the future of what was to become the family of David . . . and of Jesus.

Female statuette in clay found at Hacilar, sixth millennium. Archaeological museum of Ankara

Rahab

The story of Rahab is hardly more edifying. It takes place in the time when the Hebrews, at the end of the Exodus, arrived at the promised land. Entry to it was barred by the city of Jericho. Joshua sent two men to spy it out. They got there and went to the house of a prostitute called Rahab, where they stayed. The king of Jericho wanted to have them arrested. Rahab hid them and saved their lives (Joshua 2).

This episode, which is probably legendary, comes from a kind of work similar to those modern 'true-life stories' which show how 'bad' people come to recognize a 'good cause' and join it. The story again makes a heroine out of a prostitute, one who betrays her own people. Rahab escapes, is integrated into the people of God and becomes the mother of Boaz, himself grandfather of Jesse, father of David.

What is interesting about this story is the way in which it makes us see how the biblical revelation begins from humble and ambiguous realities. Rahab is just a woman who wants to escape the fall of her city. But more than a millennium afterwards the author of the Letter to the Hebrews reread the old story as an illustration of faith leading the pagans to salvation. He declared without hesitation, 'By faith Rahab the harlot did not perish with those who were disobedient, because she had given friendly welcome to the spies' (Hebrews 11.31). Thus one day the supreme faith emerged from what to begin with was only a basic desire to live; and Christ himself has roots in what was only a story of a prostitute visited by some Bedouins who came out of the desert.

Bathsheba

The story of Bathsheba the wife of Uriah the Hittite, seduced by David, is no less humiliating for Jewish remembrance. So much so that the book of Chronicles, which seeks to exalt the memory of God's elect, leaves it out. However, it is through adultery followed by the disguised assassination of the husband that the prestigious monarch, the basis of a whole Israelite tradition, assured the continuity of his royal house (II Samuel 11–12).

Ruth

As for the fourth wife cited by Matthew, Ruth, the Arabian woman from the country of Moab, she recalls a no less humiliating memory than the others for Jews who loudly proclaimed their superiority to neighbouring peoples. The book of Ruth was written after the return from exile at a time when, on the pretext of religious purity, Ezra was requiring Jews who had married foreign wives to send them home (Ezra 9; 10).

A narrator describes how in ancient times an Israelite who had emigrated to Moab had married a woman of the land. After his death she had returned to Bethlehem, whence her husband had come, together with her mother-in-law, Naomi. There Ruth had met Boaz, her husband's kinsman. She succeeded in getting married to him through the levirate law. Of this union Obed, David's grandfather, was born (Ruth).

In the eyes of the purist Jews this was a misalliance. A happy misalliance, the writer suggests. God does not act through our national or racist patterns.

Depiction of sodomy. First half of the second millennium BC. Louvre, Paris. *Photo J. S. Cooper and E. Lessing/Magnum*

An extract from the Decalogue, the basic law of Israel

God said, 'I am the Lord your God, who brought you out of the land of Egypt, out of the house of bondage . . .
You shall not commit adultery . . .
You shall not covet your neighbour's wife, or his manservant, or his maidservant, or his ox, or his ass, or anything that is his.'

Exodus 20.1, 14, 17

The law of Israel is a superior law

I have taught you the statutes and ordinances; keep them and do them; for that will be your wisdom and your understanding in the sight of the peoples, who, when they hear all these statutes, will say, 'Surely this great nation is a wise and understanding people . . .' And what great nation is there that has statutes and ordinances so righteous as all this law which I set before you this day?

Deuteronomy 4.6–8

A law given because of the hardness of the human heart

Into this story full of 'sound and fury' the Law, however, tries to introduce some order. It does so in the name of an ideal of freedom and justice: the God who freed his people from Egypt invites them to adopt customs and laws whose profoundly human character will win the other nations over by introducing to them the wisdom of the God of Israel.

God bans everything that undermines human life by destroying its freedom. Thus putting married life in jeopardy – stealing another person's spouse by adultery, interfering with the life

Some sexual laws in the book of Deuteronomy

If any man takes a wife, and goes in to her, and then spurns her, and charges her with shameful conduct, and brings an evil name upon her, saying, 'I took this woman, and when I came near her, I did not find in her the tokens of virginity,' then the father of the young woman and her mother shall take and bring out the tokens of her virginity to the elders of the city in the gate; and the father of the young woman shall say to the elders, 'I gave my daughter to this man to wife, and he spurns her; and lo, he has made shameful charges against her, saying, "I did not find in your daughter the tokens of virginity." And yet these are the tokens of my daughter's virginity.' And they shall spread the garment before the elders of the city. Then the elders of that city shall take the man and whip him; and they shall fine him a hundred shekels of silver, and give them to the father of the young woman, because he has brought an evil name upon a virgin of Israel; and she shall be his wife; he may not put her away all his days.

But if the thing is true, that the tokens of virginity were not found in the young woman, then they shall bring out the young woman to the door of her father's house, and the men of her city shall stone her to death with stones, because she has wrought folly in Israel by playing the harlot in her father's house; so you shall purge the evil from Israel.

If a man is found lying with the wife of another man, both of them shall die, the man who lies with the woman, and the woman. So you shall purge the evil from Israel.

If there is a betrothed virgin, and a man meets her in the city and lies with her, then you shall bring them both out to the gate of that city, and you shall stone them to death with stones, the young woman because she did not cry for help though she was in the city, and the man because he violated his neighbour's wife; so you shall purge the evil from the midst of you. But if in the open country a man meets a young woman who is betrothed, and the man seizes her and lies with her, then only the man who lay with her shall die. But to the young woman you shall do nothing; in the young woman there is no offence punishable by death . . . because he came upon her in the open country, and though the betrothed young woman cried for help there was no one to rescue her.

If a man meets a virgin who is not betrothed, and seizes her and lies with her, and they are found; then the man who lay with her shall give to the father of the young woman fifty shekels of silver, and she shall be his wife, because he has violated her; he may not put her away all his days.

Deuteronomy 22.13–29

---

of a third party by transitory sexual liaisons – is to undermine stable and balanced social relationships. Far from devaluing a married and sexual life which they surround with prohibitions, the divine commandments safeguard its true human fulfilment. Besides, this fulfilment is an aspect of encounter with God. The union of man and woman on the road to freedom matches the convenant of the people with its God, and the one relates to the other.

Some texts in Deuteronomy, a late book written after a long meditation, show a real concern for respect for the wife's rights: she is protected against male whim.

A law which favours men

However, there is a limit to the Law and even more to its 'statutes'. The woman remains above all the property of another: first father and then husband or betrothed. The 'macho' perspective which can already be felt in the original law of the Decalogue remains in the background. The simple fact that the prohibition relates above all to the rights of the male and that the wife is given the rank of an object that can be coveted shows the mentality that the legislator is trying to curb. We are still a long way from real reciprocity between the two sexes. The practice of the dowry

King
Mycerinus
and his
wife.
Boston
Museum

and the title of 'master' conferred on the husband indicate at what point the wife is totally subordinate to her husband.

The desire of the man to affirm his power and to assure his descendants is represented quite naturally by polygamy. The kings multiply their unions depending on their desires, but also out of political interests. Within their harems the interplay of rivalries can only debase real love.

The law gives the husband the right to repudiate a sterile wife. But generally speaking he is also allowed to send back a wife who proves to have a 'defect', even in Deuteronomy, though the situation there is already much more open (c.f.24.1ff.). Without doubt legislation to some degree defends the wife against male whim. But above all it favours the man. The adulterous wife and her accomplice are condemned to death by stoning, while there is no severe punishment as

Nathan's reproaches to David

Nathan went to David and said to him:
'There were two men in a certain city, the one rich and the other poor. The rich man had very many flocks and herds; but the poor man had nothing but one little ewe lamb, which he had brought. And he brought it up, and it grew up with him and with his children; it used to eat of his morsel, and drink from his cup, and lie in his bosom, and it was like a daughter to him. Now there came a traveller to the rich man, and he was unwilling to take one of his own flock or herd to prepare for the wayfarer who had come to him, but he took the poor man's lamb, and prepared it for the man who had come to him.'

Then David's anger was greatly kindled against the man; and he said to Nathan, 'As the Lord lives, the man who has done this deserves to die; and he shall restore the lamb fourfold, because he did this thing, and because he had no pity.'

Nathan said to David, 'You are the man. Thus says the Lord, the God of Israel, "I anointed you king over Israel, and I delivered you out of the hand of Saul; and I gave you your master's house, and your master's wives into your bosom, and gave you the house of Israel and of Judah; and as if this were too little, I would add to you as much more . . . But you have smitten Uriah the Hittite with the sword, and have taken his wife to be your wife . . ." Thus says the Lord, "Behold I will raise up evil against you out of your own house; and I will take your wives before your eyes, and give them to your neighbour, and he shall lie with your wives in the sight of this sun. For you did it secretly, but I will do this thing before Israel, and before the sun."'

II Samuel 12.1–13

a sanction against the husband who has sexual relationships with prostitutes.

What the story of David reveals is typical from this point of view. When the prophet Nathan goes to reproach the king for his crime he does not censure him for having increased the number of his wives: the prophet points out to the king that God has already given him an abundant harem and accuses him of having mocked the rights of another husband.

However, subsequently Nathan was to give his support over the succession to the throne to Solomon, the son of Bathsheba, who from then on is recognized as the privileged queen.

Failings are therefore clearly denounced and condemned. But they do not represent a definitive bar to the future. It is from a line which begins in guilt that the Messiah who bears the hopes of Israel will one day grow.

When a woman saves her people

'God writes straight with crooked lines,' Paul Claudel was fond of saying. God can make use of situations which to begin with have gone wrong in order to pursue his designs and lead the whole of humanity to his salvation.

It is equally striking to see how when the prophets or the book of Deuteronomy protest against the great number of royal matrimonial unions they do not do so in the name of the ideal couple presented in Genesis but because these alliances put the purity of the covenant in question. Contracted for political reasons, they allow foreign queens to introduce into Israel pagan cults and the customs associated with them.

Leaving aside the desire or the personal interest of the kings we can see on the other hand that at this stage of cultural evolution the good of the group not only transcends that of individuals but can conflict with it. From earliest antiquity parents decided whom their children were to marry. Subsequently, concern for the purity of the race would lead to the exclusion of certain alliances, or even to their dissolution (I have already mentioned the opposition of Ezra to marriages with foreigners). On the other hand the author of the book of Esther congratulates

---

The story of Esther

The book of Esther tells a very symbolic story for a people constantly threatened with extermination: the Jews deported to Susa were condemned to a real pogrom. Fortunately Mordecai, the old wise man, succeeded in introducing his niece Esther into the harem of king Ahasuerus. Esther became the king's favourite wife and succeeded in thwarting the intrigues of Haman, the enemy of the Jews, thus saving her people.

Before becoming involved in a decisive conversation with Ahasuerus, Esther made the following prayer:

Remember, O Lord; make thyself known in this time of our affliction, and give me courage, O King of the gods and Master of all dominion! Put eloquent speech in my mouth before the lion, and turn his heart to hate the man who is fighting against us, so that there may be an end of him and those who agree with him. But save us by thy hand, and help me, who am alone and have no helper but thee, O Lord. Thou hast knowledge of all things and thou knowest that I hate the splendour of the wicked and abhor the bed of the uncircumcised and of any alien. Thou knowest my necessity . . .

Esther 14.12–16

Once again, we find ourselves quite a long way from what were thought of as sacred laws – for the greater good of the people of God.

---

himself that a young Jewish woman, by becoming the favourite wife of a pagan king who had got rid of the previous queen, could have been the instrument of salvation for her people.

The affirmation of love despite the hardness of the human heart

The ruling customs and the limits of the law which channel them do not, however, take account of an infinitely more positive reality: that of an authentic love which affirms itself powerfully. The Old Testament continually offers us models of profoundly united couples. It is of Rachel, the barren one, that Jacob is especially fond (Genesis 29). Elkanah consoles Hannah, his wife, who despairs of having children: in his eyes 'she is worth more than ten sons' (I Samuel 1.8). Stories aimed at heightening the awareness of being the people protected by God, like that of Judith, or the wisdom literature, present a conjugal ideal infinitely surpassing strict law. The exclusiveness of certain unions is praised (one has only to recall the vivid and tender description the prophet gives of Bathsheba, 'the one lamb'). There is praise for a faithfulness based on love which can outlast death. There is a celebration of fidelity towards the 'love of one's youth'. There

Etruscan statuette in bronze. Couple. End of seventh century BC. Louvre, Paris. *Photo Chezeville*

'The thing comes from the Lord'

Abraham ordered his servant to go to Mesopotamia to look for a wife for his son Isaac from his own race. Having met the young Rebekah by the fountain, the servant thought that he had found the wife he was looking for. He asked Laban, Rebekah's brother, and Bethuel, her father, for permission for her to be married. They replied:

'The thing comes from the Lord; we cannot speak to you bad or good. Behold, Rebekah is before you, take her and go, and let her be the wife of your master's son, as the Lord has spoken . . .'

The next day Rebekah's parents wanted to keep her several days longer, but the servant said to them 'Do not delay me, since the Lord has prospered my way; let me go that I may go to my master.' They called Rebekah and said to her, 'Will you go with this man?' She said, 'I will go.'

They blessed Rebekah and said to her, 'Our sister, be the mother of thousands of ten thousands; and may your descendants possess the gate of those who hate them!'

Then Rebekah and her maids arose, and rode upon the camels and followed the man; thus the servant took Rebekah, and went his way.

Now Isaac went out to meditate in the field in the evening; and he lifted up his eyes and looked, and behold, there were camels coming. And Rebekah lifted up her eyes, and when she saw Isaac, she alighted from the camel, and said to the servant, 'Who is the man yonder, walking in the field to meet us?' The servant said, 'It is my master.' So she took her veil and covered herself. And the servant told Isaac all the things that he had done. Then Isaac brought her into the tent, and took Rebekah, and she became his wife; and he loved her.

Genesis 24

Rough draft of a sculpture representing Nefertiti and Akhenaton. Brooklyn museum

Marriage as seen by a wise man of Israel

Happy is the husband of a good wife;
the number of his days shall be doubled.
A loyal wife rejoices her husband, and he will complete his
years in peace.
A good wife is a great blessing;
she will be granted among the blessings of the man who
fears the Lord.
Whether rich or poor, his heart is glad,
and at all times his face is cheerful.

Like the sun rising in the heights of the Lord,
so is the beauty of a good wife in her well-ordered home.
Like the shining lamp on the holy lampstand,
so is a beautiful face on a stately figure.

Sirach 26.1–4, 16–17

is stress on the way in which a true mother of a family can be a full partner to her husband.

It is above all in the Song of Songs that the dynamism of an unconstrained love is affirmed in all its force. That Judaism was able to integrate into its sacred books such a free expression of eroticism, that it interpreted the game of hide and seek among lovers as the expression of the relationship between God and humanity, shows that the crudeness of marital customs could not extinguish the real sparkle of love and that love

Bust of Queen Nefertiti. Berlin. *Photo Boudot Lamotte*

'The voice of my beloved'

The voice of my beloved!
Behold, he comes,
leaping over the mountains,
bounding over the hills.
My beloved is like a gazelle,
or a young stag.
My beloved speaks and says to me:
'Arise, my love, my fair one, and come away.
O my dove, in the clefts of the rock,
in the covert of the cliff,
let me see your face,
let me hear your voice,
for your voice is sweet,
and your face is comely.
. . . My beloved is mine and I am his.
Set me as a seal upon your heart,
as a seal upon your arm;
for love is strong as death,
jealousy is cruel as the grave.
Its flashes are flashes of fire,
a most vehement flame.
Many waters cannot quench love,
neither can floods drown it.
If a man offered for love
all the wealth of his house,
it would be utterly scorned.

Song of Solomon 2.8–16; 8.6–7

---

far surpasses the official legislation of an age.

Jewish piety came to see marriage as something sacred, corresponding to the divine vocation of humanity. The little moralizing tale which we have in the form of the book of Tobit is concerned to stress that the union of Tobias and Sarah is to be seen as a real exorcism against the demons of sensuality, which destroy humanity. But despite its deprecation of desire, which is difficult for modern men and women to understand, the prayer of the young couple on their wedding night shows a profound awareness of the sacred character of married union.

It was only possible to produce such a story

The wedding night of Tobias and Sarah

The parents went out and shut the door. Tobias got up from the bed and said to Sarah, 'Sister, get up and let us pray that the Lord may have mercy upon us.' She got up and they began to pray for protection, and he began: 'Blessed art thou, O God of our fathers, and blessed be thy holy and glorious name for ever. Let the heavens and all thy creatures bless thee. Thou madest Adam and gavest him Eve his wife as a helper and support.

From them the race of mankind has sprung. Thou didst say, "It is not good that the man should be alone; let us make a helper for him like himself." And now, O Lord, I am not taking this sister of mine because of lust, but with sincerity. Grant that I may find mercy and may grow old together with her!'

Tobit 8.5–7

because, contrary to the dominant customs and independently of official law, Judaism had already become profoundly aware that the love of man and woman has a real spiritual significance.

They shall be one flesh

Extended over the centuries, Jewish meditation on the significance of marriage finds particularly rich expression in the Book of Genesis. In its account of the origin of the world and the people of God this book gives us the fruits of a long experience which allow us to see God's original plan for married life: appealing to ancient traditions which were read and meditated on for a long time, it affirms that there is a profound parallel between the covenant of God with his people and that which binds man and wife.

In Genesis 2.18–25, taking up a very old story the written form of which goes back to about 2000 BC, the author who gave the final form to the first books of the Bible, in about the fifth century BC, presents a pictorial account of the creation of the first couple. Having fashioned the man from clay and breathed into him the breath of life, God says, 'It is not good for man to be alone. I must create a helpmeet to be with him.' And in order to finish his work, which is still imperfect, he detaches one of Adam's ribs and makes woman from it. Then Adam cries out, 'Bone of my bone and flesh of my flesh! She shall be called woman (in Hebrew *isshah*) for she was drawn from man (*ish*).' And the author of the story adds: 'That is why a man leaves his father and mother and joins his wife, and they become one flesh. And they were both naked, the man and the woman, and they were not ashamed.'

To say that the man is superior to the woman because he was created first is as vain as to exalt the woman as the crown of the species.

The essential point is that the text affirms unity in difference. The human being only finds fulfilment in encounter with another. Man is torn from the torpor which would have been his had he remained alone in the womb of paradise. The possibility of love is the beginning of spiritual adventure, which takes place in dialogue.

But this adventure presupposes a break. 'The man will leave his father and his mother . . .' For the mother, the one who gives life, can also be the one who holds it back: the lost paradise towards which one is always tempted to return to find haven there when the trials of existence become too hard; the object of the dream of a return to a bygone past which there is an unconscious quest to rediscover in all kinds of forms. As for the father, the one who procreates and allows the child to form itself, he can also become the being who bars the way to the future: the symbol of prohibitions, he then reflects the threatening God whom we are all tempted to imagine when seized with anxiety in the face of an unknown future.

But the true God makes humanity open to its future by inviting men and women to love. By tearing aside what could shut up or bar the way, he frees his creature.

God says, 'Be fruitful, multiply, fill the earth and subdue it.'

From now on the world is given to the man and the woman. They in turn are invited to create. The first expression of a creative opening to the future is the child. But this work is put in a wider framework: the humanization of a universe that man is charged to order by his language and his action.

So the sexual condition expresses and makes concrete the essential vocation of humanity, 'being for the other', called to find life through the other. And through the other he is fertile. In this way he responds to God's call.

The Kiss, Brancusi, 1908. Musée national d'art moderne, Paris. *Photo Giraudon*

What is at the heart of married life, fear or trust?

The Creation, Hieronymus Bosch. Detail. God brings together Adam and Eve. Prado museum, Madrid. *Photo Giraudon*

'By faith' Abraham responded to God's call. Leaving the land in which he had grown up, he departed, taking with him his wife, Sarah, his nephew and his goods: that is the Christian commentary on the vocation of the ancestor of the people of God (Hebrews 11.8).

It is through the brief description in Genesis 12.1–4 that the biblical author introduces to us a man who at last accepts his calling and sets out on the way of life, instead of shutting himself up in his closed universe. But this man is not an isolated individual; he has a wife and he has a family.

However, the contradiction is far from having disappeared from the heart of the one who has resumed dialogue with his God. Abraham is certainly waiting for the country that he has been promised. But at the same time he dreams of attaining by himself firm ground which will at last give him a feeling of security. The fear of oblivion and the desire for tangible certainty thus explain two episodes connected with him. In fact through these episodes the editor of Genesis expresses his meditation on the destiny of his people and of humanity. These two stories raise questions about the bond between Abraham and Sarah. They show how sin is a permanent reality in life, threatening all human attitudes and in particular making the marriage bond fragile.

The first text shows what sexual relationship becomes when the husband does not take responsibility for it. The second shows how this relationship can be falsified by a legalism which obscures a very instinctive aspect of desire.

When the husband denies his bond with his wife

The Book of Genesis (12.10–20) tells how the ancestor of the chosen people, Abraham, had to go down to Egypt with his family to escape famine.

When he was about to enter Egypt, Abraham said to his wife Sarah, 'I know that you are a woman beautiful to behold; and when the Egyptians see you, they will say, "This is his wife"; then they will kill me, but they will let you live. Say you are my sister, that it may go well with me because of you, and that my life may be spared on your account.'

This story describes a temptation which puts in question the bond between husband and wife, and by the same token the inner equilibrium of any human being.

In former times, as today, when a husband was disturbed about his future he was tempted to reject his real bond with a wife in order to save what he thought his life was. This was – and is – to give the 'masculine' values of efficiency and rationality priority over feminine values which are said to be sources of weaknss. It is to destroy the fertile polarity of the two sexes not only in marriage but also in society. Thus Abraham denies that Sarah is his wife, i.e. a part of himself: 'Say you are my sister . . .' But, at the same time he reduces her to being no more than a sexual object through which he hopes to secure himself a tangible advantage: 'That it may go well with me because of you.'

In fact, by separating himself from half of himself (some modern psychologists would say, from his 'anima') the man mutilates himself, just as he mutilates the woman who ratifies the negation of her being by submitting to male demands.

However, God cannot accept this break in the marriage tie. Sarah is restored to her husband who has to acknowledge his fault and make a public confession that his companion is indeed his wife. It is a strange thing that in another story, in Genesis 20.14, it is even said that Abimelek, who has ravished Sarah, seized with remorse because of his unwitting adultery, is not content with chiding the patriarch for his lie. As he restores his wife to him, he heaps up goods on him. Thus the story gives a symbolic indication that, far from perishing because of his wife, a husband is enriched when he acknowledges who she really is. He can resume his way. The future opens up again.

When a man only considers his wife as a remedy for his fear of oblivion

The second episode centres on a child.

For the Semite, who had not yet arrived at the idea of resurrection, only a male child gave the father the feeling of surviving himself and prolonging himself in another. Abraham dreams of numerous posterity. Has not God promised this to him? However, the patriarch is old, like his spouse, who is also barren. So how can he put any trust in a word which seems incapable of realization? The patriarch therefore uses a stratagem recognized by the marriage law of his time, one which he is advised to adopt by his wife, who is concerned for her husband's interests: he will have a son by a slave and the boy will receive full rights as legitimate heir. But this offspring of a human concern determined by a desire to survive, and therefore closed to the freedom of the promise, will not assure Abraham of the life to which he has been called. The true son must be conceived in faith. Finally Ishmael, the son of Hagar, the slave girl, has to give place to Isaac, the gift of God, son of the barren woman (Genesis 16.18).

It does not matter much here how historical the tradition was on which the biblical writer

From the very beginnings of the people of God one can see a denunciation of certain ambiguities in the relationship between husband and wife. This relationship cannot be subordinated to the desire for human security, even if this is based on law. It can only be the source of life if it is filled with confidence. Fear leads nowhere. Only faith can bear the future.

Thus, like the first, this second episode relativizes the most spontaneous human perspectives on marriage. It is not just a physical thing; it is a spiritual reality.

God reveals a new dimension of love

With the prophets Hosea, Jeremiah, Ezekiel and Isaiah a new dimension of human love is affirmed. Its true model is the love that God bears his people and, through him, all humanity.

For the Lord loves Israel freely, as husband and wife must love each other. At his people's side God is involved in a history which, through the most profound crises, leads to the fullness of the encounter between the creature and its creator.

God and the unfaithful wife

In a paradoxical way, this idea is confirmed by the misery of a ridiculed husband, Hosea. The prophet married a wife who proved to be a prostitute. He began by rejecting the children which he had had by her; then he decided to repudiate her. But through his suffering he sees how God may feel on being deceived by the people of Israel, who are compared to a beloved spouse. So, discovering the free character of the

meditated for so long. The essential thing is the affirmation of the fundamental value of the faith of which the child is the sign. Descendants must not be thought of in terms of security. They only become truly spiritual, bearing the divine promise, to the degree to which they are marked with the character of free gift.

God and the unfaithful wife

Beginning from his own experience of a love capable of forgiving the wife who had cheated him, Hosea made God speak to the Israelites like this:

Plead with your mother, plead –
for she is not my wife,
and I am not her husband –
that she put away her harlotry from her face,
and her adultery from between her breasts;
lest I strip her naked
and make her as in the day she was born,
and make her like a wilderness,
and set her like a parched land,
and slay her with thirst.
Upon her children also I will have no pity,
because they are children of harlotry . . .

She shall pursue her lovers; but not overtake them;
and she shall seek them, but shall not find them.

Then she shall say, 'I will go and return to my first
*   husband,*
for it was better with me then than now.'
And she did not know that it was I who gave her
the grain, the wine and the oil . . .
Therefore, behold, I will allure her,
and bring her into the wilderness,
and speak tenderly to her . . .
And there she shall answer as in the days of her youth,
as at the time when she came out of the land of Egypt . . .
And I will betroth you to me for ever;
I will betroth you to me in righteousness and in justice,
in steadfast love, and in mercy.
I will betroth you to me in faithfulness;
and you shall know the Lord.

Hosea 2.2–4, 7–8, 14–15, 19–20

My people are bent on turning away from me . . .
How can I give you up, O Ephraim!
How can I hand you over, O Israel! . . .
My heart recoils within me,
my compassion grows warm and tender.
I will not execute my fierce anger,
I will not again destroy Ephraim,
for I am God and not man,
the Holy One in your midst,
and I will not come to destroy.

Hosea 11.7–9

love which the Lord continues to bear his people, despite their faults, he understands the overwhelming significance of fidelity. He then decides to take back his wife and forgive her. After a time of purification, of 'return to the desert', she will prove capable of recognizing the merciful goodness of her husband and respond to him by her own fidelity.

Jeremiah takes up the same nuptial symbolism and contrasts the corruption and the betrayal of Israel, the unfaithful bride, with the eternal love of God for his people, before announcing the reconciliation and the new covenant which will come to change the human heart.

Even more brutally, Ezekiel illustrates the conduct of the people of God by comparing it to an abandoned girl baby, rescued by her Lord, brought up in splendour, loved, but escaping her benefactor to prostitute herself with strangers (pagan people). However, the day will come when the cheated husband will himself come to restore the destroyed alliance.

Finally, the second part of Isaiah, the book of the consolation of Israel written towards the end of the time of the Babylonian exile, can proclaim in a revolutionary way: 'Do not be ashamed. Do not be confounded . . . For your Maker is your husband . . . Does one repudiate the wife of youth? For a brief moment I forsook you . . . But with everlasting love I will have compassion on you' (Isaiah 54.4–8).

Here we can see the dissolution of the pattern of a social pact based on a contract of a commercial kind aimed at providing security. What is affirmed is love in total freedom; it is mercy capable of getting over all deceptions in an attempt ultimately to arouse a loving response. The worst conflicts remain full of hope; the most serious misunderstandings are still open to the future, to this 'new covenant' which Jeremiah, in the depths of the night in which he was tragically caught up, saw would one day transfigure the world.

The symbolic history of Jerusalem

Again the word of the Lord came to me: 'Son of man, make known to Jerusalem her abominations, and say, Thus says the Lord God to Jerusalem: Your origin and your birth are of the land of the Canaanites; your father was an Amorite, and your mother a Hittite. And as for your birth, on the day you were born your navel string was not cut, nor were you washed with water to cleanse you, nor rubbed with salt, nor swathed with bands. No eye pitied you, to do any of these things to you out of compassion for you; but you were cast out on the open field, for you were abhorred, on the day that you were born.

And when I passed by you, and saw you weltering in your blood, I said to you in your blood, "Live, and grow up like a plant of the field." And you grew up and became tall and arrived at full maidenhood; your breasts were formed, and your hair had grown; yet you were naked and bare.

When I passed by you again and looked upon you, behold, you were at the age for love; and I spread my skirt over you, and covered your nakedness: yea, I plighted my troth to you and entered into a covenant with you, says the Lord God, and you became mine. Then I bathed you with water and washed off your blood from you and anointed you with oil. I clothed you also with embroidered cloth and shod you with leather, I swathed you in fine linen and covered you with silk. And I decked you with ornaments, and put bracelets on your arms, and a chain on your neck. And I put a ring on your nose, and earrings in your ears, and a beautiful crown on your head . . . And your renown went forth among the nations because of your beauty, for it was perfect through the splendour which I had bestowed upon you, says the Lord God.

But you trusted in your beauty, and played the harlot because of your renown, and lavished your harlotries on any passer-by. You took some of your garments, and made for yourself gaily decked shrines, and on them played the harlot . . .

How lovesick is your heart, says the Lord God, seeing you did all these things, the deeds of a brazen harlot . . . Adulterous wife, who receives strangers instead of her husband! Men give gifts to all harlots but you gave your gifts to all your lovers, bribing them to come to you from every side for your harlotries. So you were different from other women in your harlotries: none solicited you to play the harlot; and you gave hire, while no hire was given to you; therefore you were different.'

Wherefore, O harlot, hear the word of the Lord: Thus says the Lord God, Because your shame was laid bare and your nakedness uncovered in your harlotries with your lovers, and because of all your idols, and because of the blood of your children that you gave to them, therefore, behold, I will gather all your lovers with whom you took pleasure, all those you loved and all those you loathed; I will gather them against you from every side, and will uncover your nakedness to them, that they may see all your nakedness. And I will judge you as women who break wedlock and shed blood are judged, and bring upon you the blood of wrath and jealousy. And I will give you into the hand of your lovers . . .

Yea, thus says the Lord God: I will deal with you as you have done, who have despised the oath in breaking the covenant, yet I will remember my covenant with you in the days of your youth, and I will establish with you an everlasting covenant. Then you will remember your ways, and be ashamed . . . I will establish my covenant with you, and you shall know that I am the Lord, that you may remember and be confounded, and never open your mouth again because of your shame, when I forgive you all that you have done, says the Lord God.'

Ezekiel 16

3
Marriage in the New Testament

Jesus and marriage

A new perspective on the family

Filled with the love of the one whom he called his Father, raised up by the Spirit, Jesus came to proclaim the kingdom. Specifically his purpose was to bring to birth, through the people of Israel, a new people, the family of the children of God.

This perspective leads Jesus to relativize human realities. Work, riches, and even married love and the family only take on their true meaning as a result of their relationship to the new reality which arises, in the holy people, moulded by divine love, which he has come to create.

That is why he asks those who, like himself, will take the road to proclaim the kingdom, to renounce their families. But at the same time he promises them that they will rediscover a hundredfold what they seem to have lost (Mark 10.28–30). From now on, they will in fact be part of a new family, held together by the same faith.

True love in the perspective of Jesus

Jesus does not pay special attention to the love of man and woman. This is only one particular way of living out the great law of love which is that of all those who live in the perspective of the kingdom of God. The husband and wife are the 'closest neighbours'.

A Pharisee tries to embarrass Jesus by asking him, 'Master, what is the greatest commandment of the Law?' Jesus replies, 'You shall love the Lord your God with all your heart and all your mind and all your strength; that is the first and great commandment. And the second is like it: you shall love your neighbour as yourself. On these two commandments hang all the law and the prophets' (Matt. 22.34–39).

Jesus himself lived out his relationship to others, and particularly to women, in an amazingly new way. At a time when, socially and religiously, women were considered to be inferior beings, he showed how he was entirely at ease with them, recognizing them completely as neighbours and giving them a place among his disciples. He, the celibate, demonstrated the possibility of perfectly clear vision. Purity *par excellence* can then raise up the despised sinner and affirm that much will be forgiven her because she loved much. It acquits the woman caught in adultery from the condemn-

Forgiveness for the woman who was a sinner

One of the Pharisees asked Jesus to eat with him, and he went into the Pharisee's house, and sat at table. And behold, a woman of the city, who was a sinner, when she learned that he was sitting at table in the Pharisee's house, brought an alabaster flask of ointment, and standing behind him at his feet, weeping, she began to wet his feet with her tears, and wiped them with the hair of her head, and kissed his feet, and anointed them with the ointment.

Now when the Pharisee who had invited him saw it, he said to himself, 'If this man were a prophet, he would have known who and what sort of woman this is who is touching him, for she is a sinner.' And Jesus answering said to him, 'Simon, I have something to say to you.' And he answered, 'What is it, Teacher?' 'A certain creditor had two debtors; and owed five hundred denarii, and the other fifty. When they could not pay, he forgave them both. Now which of them will love him more?' Simon answered, 'The one, I suppose, to whom he forgave more.' And he said to him, 'You have judged rightly.'

Then turning toward the woman he said to Simon, 'Do you see this woman? I entered your house, you gave me no water for my feet, but she has wet my feet with her tears and wiped them with her hair. You gave me no kiss, but from the time I came in she has not ceased to kiss my feet. You did not anoint my head with oil, but she has anointed my feet with ointment. Therefore I tell you, her sins, which are many, are forgiven, for she loved much; but he who is forgiven little, loves little.'

Luke 7.36–47

ation of those who thought that they could mark their own deep guilt by projecting it on to a woman who had been marginalized by the law.

Living in the perspective of the kingdom, where all is subordinated to the coming of God in the world, Jesus can even suggest that marriage should be seen in terms of the horizon which it opens up. In this way he gives marriage its real meaning by integrating it into an overall plan of life. That is what he does in addressing the great majority of his disciples.

For beside the itinerant disciples who had left all to follow him, Jesus had other members of his movement, who stayed where they were. He did not ask them to leave everything. However, he did call on them to live their everyday life in a radically new way. In so doing he recognized the full value of married life and the family, showing how, when these are seen and lived in the Spirit of the kingdom, they find a definitive meaning in God.

So he can denounce the deep vice hidden behind the legalism of the Pharisees who have come hypocritically to ask him about the application of the Mosaic law on divorce:

'It is by reason of the hardness of your heart that Moses has written this prescription for you. But from the origin of creation he made them man and women. So the man shall leave his father and mother and the two shall be one flesh. So what God has put together man may not separate' (Mark 10.5–10; Matthew 19.4–7).

All is up with a marriage in which the contract is only a function of the interest that the man has in it. In married life each partner becomes responsible for the other, on the route of human adventure leading to God. In the perspective of the kingdom, it is an irreversible commitment, since through it something even more essential is at stake: the relationship to the one who is the source of love.

An image of God's love for his people

Jesus himself provides the model for being responsible for others. Just beneath the surface of their story, in accord with prophetic symbolism, the evangelists present him as the husband coming to realize the marriage between God and humanity in his own person. That in particular is the meaning of the wedding feast of Cana and the miracle of the water changed into wine: in telling this story John gives symbolic expression to the profound change of spiritual regime that Jesus comes to inaugurate. In the question by which he responds to the request of his mother, Christ shows the enormous gap which there is between a perspective that is still limited and his own: he is utterly intent on the hour of his marriage with humanity, which will be accomplished on the cross. So he can change the water of Jewish ritual ablutions into new wine: the regime of the law gives place to that of the free gift of love.

The Gospels do not tell us more about Jesus' view of marriage. But 'he that has ears to hear let him hear': it is for the believer to discover the practical significance of his good news. In the suggestion that all human reality should be seen in the light of the God of love who reveals himself in the mystery of Easter, he has opened up a new perspective on marriage itself. It is for his disciples to draw the conclusions!

The woman caught in adultery

The scribes and the Pharisees brought a woman who had been caught in adultery, and placing her in the midst they said to him, 'Teacher, this woman has been caught in the act of adultery. Now in the law Moses commanded us to stone such. What do you say about her?' This they said to test him, that they might have some charge to bring against him. Jesus bent down and wrote with his finger on the ground. And as they continued to ask him, he stood up and said to them, 'Let him who is without sin among you be the first to throw a stone at her.' And once more he bent down and wrote with his finger on the ground. But when they heard it, they went away, one by one, beginning with the eldest, and Jesus was left alone with the woman standing before him. Jesus looked up and said to her, 'Woman, where are they? Has no one condemned you?' She said, 'No one, Lord.' And Jesus said, 'Neither do I condemn you; go, and do not sin again.'

John 8.3–11

The Marriage at Cana. Italian school, fifteenth century. *Photo Giraudon*

Marriage in Paul's perspective

It is in the letters of Paul that we find the deepest reflection on marriage. However, it would be a mistake to go straight to the texts about marital problems without putting the apostle's reflections in the general context of his vision of the renewal of life introduced by Jesus.

In the Letter to the Romans Paul censures both Jews and Gentiles: both are equally under the sign of 'the divine anger', because both are guilty. The former have not understood the inner law of their heart; failing to recognize the true God, they have succumbed to concupiscence and have been delivered over to impurity and debauchery in all its forms, as is clear from their sexual customs. However, he is just as blunt to the latter, who boast that they have the divine law which gives them a superior position from which to judge the former: 'You who judge these faults harshly and commit them, can you expect to escape the divine judgment?' (Romans 2.3).

What Paul essentially reproaches the Jews for is having often forgotten the free gift of the divine love and having behaved towards God according to a commercial mentality bound up with a legalistic vision of the covenant. They claim to have a right to the divine love, and thus to the advantages which flow from it. In so doing they demonstrate the hardness of their hearts.

The one who lives by faith finds a way into quite a different spiritual universe. Filled with the divine spirit, he or she escapes the mentality of the 'old man' and enters into the world of the only true and durable love, that of which God himself has shown us the model in the crucified Jesus.

The apostle can then declare to the Corinthians: 'I feel a divine jealousy for you, for I betrothed you to Christ to present you as a pure bride to her husband' (II Corinthians 11.2).

That is the global perspective from which he views the problem of marriage: he sees it as a participation in the radiation of the free love of God manifested in Jesus Christ.

Marriage and virginity

Following his master's example, Paul himself renounced married life to devote himself entirely to his mission. He was overwhelmed by the urgency of the kingdom of God whose final coming he believes to be near.

That is why his first and most spontaneous reaction to a question about marriage from the Corinthians is to wish that his correspondents could accept celibacy in order to give themselves totally to the most urgent task: preparation for the new world which is to come. In a way he suggests that they should sacrifice everything to fight for it. But he has an equal recognition of the value of love and he defends the value of married life against certain Greek tendencies to deprecate marriage. So he refuses to insist on observation of the celibacy which he has chosen for the service of the kingdom.

He then establishes the principle of a total reciprocity between the power of the husband over his wife and that of the wife over her husband.

In the Greek world it was customary for the

Arnolfini and
his Wife,
van Eyck.
The National
Gallery,
London.
Photo Bulloz.
This painting
amounts to a
summary of
all Christian
symbolism of
marriage

43

Paul's view of marriage and virginity at the beginning of his ministry

It is well for a man not to touch a woman. But because of the temptation to immorality, each man should have his own wife and each woman her own husband. The husband should give to his wife her conjugal rights, and likewise the wife to her husband. For the wife does not rule over her own body, but the husband does; likewise the husband does not rule over his own body, but the wife does. Do not refuse one another except perhaps by agreement for a season, that you may devote yourselves to prayer; but then come together again, lest Satan tempt you through lack of self-control. I say this by way of concession, not of command. I wish that all were as I myself am. But each has his own special gift from God, one of one kind and one of another . . .

To the married I give charge, not I but the Lord, that the wife should not separate from her husband (but if she does, let her remain single or else be reconciled to her husband) and that the husband should not divorce his wife.

I Corinthians 7.1–12

husband to purchase his wife in order to have legitimate children by her. But often, too, the man sought intellectual fulfilment with courtesans and physical satisfaction in homosexual relationships. So Paul's position seemed quite revolutionary.

In offering the possibility for both Christian women and Christian men to remain virgins, he established that they were both basically equal. He gave the woman a function in terms of the kingdom, in other words in her own right, instead of just considering her a function of her sexual relationship to her husband (cf. I Corinthians 7.25ff.).

The problem of 'mixed' marriage

Finally, through his reflections on a marriage in which only one partner is a believer, Paul shows the profound motivation behind his thought: marriage is always seen in terms of its place in the history of salvation. It is because marriage makes it possible to go forward towards the fullness of life that it is itself life-giving. For the pagan spouse, the Christian can be a source of life and grace. But if the common life of a convert and a husband who has remained a pagan proves impossible, marriage loses its meaning and Paul accepts its dissolution.

This is a great mystery

The Letter to the Ephesians, written some years later, introduces a new element. The perspective of the imminent return of the Lord becomes blurred. It is no longer possible to be content with an occasional reflection on marriage. The author of the letter envisages marriage in the context of a general perspective on the growth of 'the body of Christ'. So he develops an infinitely more positive and richer point of view than that of the Letter to the Corinthians. The love of man and woman ceases to be any handicap to the coming of the kingdom. On the contrary, it is a

Called to live in peace

If any brother has a wife who is an unbeliever, and she consents to live with him, he should not divorce her. If any woman has a husband who is an unbeliever, and he consents to live with her, she should not divorce him. For the unbelieving husband is consecrated through his wife, and the unbelieving wife is consecrated through her husband. Otherwise, your children would be unclean, but as it is they are holy. But if the unbelieving partner desires to separate, let it be so; in such a case the brother or sister is not bound. For God has called us to peace. Wife, how do you know whether you will save your husband? Husband, how do you know whether you will save your wife?

I Corinthians 7.12–16

way of showing its reality. Taking up the prophetic symbolism that we find below the surface of the gospel, it establishes a parallelism between the marital relationship and the covenant of God with human beings in Jesus Christ.

We may well still be surprised at some of the directions which this text takes. Does it not take for granted the mentality which affirms the superiority of the man over the woman? It is true that no religious reflection can possibly be above the thought-patterns of a particular period. But if we remember that in the perspective of the Gospels power is simply a responsibility which accrues from service, the call of this letter would seem to be an invitation to do full justice to the role of the woman, and not to keep her in perpetual subjection.

What is interesting about this passage is that it

As Christ loved the church

Be subject to one another out of reverence for Christ. Wives, be subject to your husbands, as to the Lord. For the husband is the head of the wife as Christ is the head of the church, his body, and is himself its Saviour. As the church is subject to Christ, so let wives also be subject in everything to their husbands. Husbands, love your wives, as Christ loved the church and gave himself up for her, that he might sanctify her, having cleansed her by the washing of water with the word, that the church might be presented before him in splendour, without spot or wrinkle or any such thing, that she might be holy and without blemish. Even so husbands should love their wives as their own bodies. He who loves his wife loves himself. For no man ever hates his own flesh, but nourishes and cherishes it, as Christ does the church, because we are members of his body. For this reason a man shall leave his father and mother and be joined to his wife, and the two shall become one. This is a great mystery, and I take it to mean Christ and the church; however, let each one of you love his wife as himself, and let the wife see that she respects her husband.

Ephesians 5.21–33

takes up the original perspective of Genesis on the human couple. But it reinterprets it in the light of the new covenant, which Jesus fulfilled by coming to share in humanity and raising up the church.

'It is a great *mystery*,' said Paul. He used this term mystery to denote the whole of the divine work in which the believer thenceforward finds himself or herself involved by virtue of faith. It is clear that in the Christian perspective marriage is taken to be a sign pointing to the activity of God in Jesus Christ. So the Christian must live out married life in the Easter perspective: love, lived in faith, allows him or her to see the love of God, manifested in Jesus Christ, the one who loved to the point of sacrificing himself and giving his life. He is also the one who gives life in the perspective of this love which is that of God himself, by living it to the full. In married life one should be able to recognize the reflection of the free love of the Lord. It is by revealing in his Son the way in which he loves that God shows what must be the union between husband and wife. This spiritual perspective shatters the spontaneous human perspective.

Love can grow from the flesh, that is to say from desire and sentiment, just as Jesus was born from a physical line of descent. But there is a break in his genealogy: the birth of Jesus is the fruit of the Spirit. In the same way, the one who loves spontaneously and humanly is called to make a leap. He or she must accept being made fruitful and transformed by the divine Spirit: this is the necessary condition for escaping his or her contradictions and being 'anchored on the rock' (Matthew 7.24–28), i.e. being saved. Where the spontaneous human impulse is to think only of certainty, advantage and satisfaction, God comes to suggest gift, trust, going forward in faith and absolute fidelity. That certainly implies risk, effort, death to oneself. But it is also the source of life. It is possible salvation.

In practice the relationship between husband and wife is a particular instance, emotionally the richest there can be, of universal prescriptions relating to relationships with others, which Paul has described in his magnificent hymn to love.

Hymn to love

If I speak in the tongues of men and of angels, but have not love, I am a noisy gong or a clanging cymbal. And if I have prophetic powers, and understand all mysteries and all knowledge, and if I have all faith, so as to remove mountains, but have not love, I am nothing. If I give away all that I have, and if I deliver my body to be burned, but have not love, I gain nothing.

Love is patient and kind; love is not jealous or boastful; it is not arrogant or rude. Love does not insist on its own way, it is not irritable or resentful; it does not rejoice at wrong, but rejoices in the right. Love bears all things, believes all things, hopes all things, endures all things.

I Corinthians 13.1–7

4

Through History, the Church becomes aware of the Dimensions of Marriage

Through the revelation of the new world inaugurated by Jesus, believers are invited to discover the whole scope of their love and the need to save it from its contradictions by steeping it in the love they receive from God. But it took lengthy experience and confrontation with very different situations for the church to be able to develop this perspective. Time was needed to grasp all the possible implications of the nucleus of a new understanding introduced by the message of Jesus.

In the primitive church, the call to holy married life

The first Christians would not have dreamed of talking about the 'sacrament' of marriage in the precise sense that we give to the term sacrament today. But that does not mean that they did not experience the reality behind the term: in the perspective of the kingdom of God announced by Jesus the whole of everyday life is transfigured, but it is not thought necessary to make a methodical list of all the new riches.

In this sense the primitive church is a continuation of the Judaism from which it inherits.

So no one saw any need to 'get married in church'. In the earliest writings there is no trace of the religious celebration of marriage. Nor do we find one in the second century. In the framework of a church which today we would describe as a basic community, Ignatius of Antioch invites those who come up against problems over their marriage to ask the bishop for advice. By virtue of his knowledge of the persons concerned the bishop is then to try to resolve problems as well as possible in the circumstances by virtue of his pastoral role.

So the commitment of the couple in marriage was celebrated according to family rites and the laws of the city. The church was content to take note of a union which was normally celebrated outside it. It is only in the fourth century that Ambrose of Milan refers to a rite of putting the veil on a new bride.

A wedding in Palestine in the first century

It is the occasion for a great festival for the whole family circle. There is dancing and singing. The bridegroom goes to look for his bride to take her home; that usually means to his family: coming to live with her parents-in-law cannot always have been very easy for the bride. It is the last day in her life when she has the right not to have a veil on her head. There does not seem to have been any special religious ceremony, except for a blessing pronounced by the father of the bride. The real blessing will come with the children who are born of this union. It is not that God is not involved; on the contrary, he was thought to be the one who decided on all marriages. But since the whole life of the Jew is focussed on God, this eminently human act is holy in itself, without needing more.

By marriage the bride passes from total submission to her father to an almost total submission to her husband.

La Palestine au temps de Jesus, Cahiers Evangile 27, Du Cerf.

A human reality lived with God

Believers experience the same natural reality as unbelievers, but they are invited to live it out differently, in the framework of the church, a real small 'alternative society' of which we find some reflection in certain present-day community groups. Married life is seen spontaneously as one of the ways of living concretely in the love of Christ.

From the beginning of the third century St Clement of Alexandria, defending marriage against the Gnostics, i.e. the representatives of sects succumbing to speculations which were often marked by scorn for earthly realities, stresses that beyond sexual union and procreation, the married union is a form of spiritual union between the married couple united by God (*Stromateis III, 10, 68*).

For ever

So Christians contrast markedly with the rest of society by virtue of the seriousness with which

The Letter to Diognetus (second century?)

Christians cannot be distinguished from the rest of the human race by country or language or customs. They do not live in cities of their own; they do not use a peculiar form of speech; they do not follow an eccentric manner of life . . . They live in Greek and barbarian cities alike, as each man's lot has been cast, and follow the customs of the country in clothing and food and other matters of daily living, at the same time they give proof of the remarkable and admittedly extraordinary constitution of their own commonwealth.

They live in their own countries, but only as aliens. They have a share in everything as citizens, and endure everything as foreigners. Every foreign land is their fatherland and yet for them every fatherland is a foreign land. They marry, like everyone else, and they beget children, but they do not cast out their offspring. They share their board with each other, but not their marriage bed. It is true that they are 'in the flesh', but they do not live 'according to the flesh'. They busy themselves on earth, but their citizenship is in heaven. They obey the established laws, but in their own lives they go far beyond what the laws require.

In *Early Christian Fathers*, LCC I, SCM Press and Westminster Press 1953.

---

they take their commitment in marriage. They see in it above all the dimension of fidelity.

This fidelity is developed to the point that there is considerable reluctance to envisage remarriage after a partner is widowed. The experience of a love lived in faith takes on eternal value. So why renew it? At a time when people were still very preoccupied with the return of the Lord, was it not better to devote oneself entirely to God?

Perfection or mercy towards sinners?

In fact the church was torn between what seemed to it to be the ideal and realism. St Paul already criticizes young widows who want to remarry 'thus deserving to be condemned for having failed in their first commitment'; but a little later, aware of the difficulties, he declares: 'So I would have younger widows marry, bear children, rule their households, and not give the enemy any occasion to revile us.' For him the 'true widows' are those who have been the wife of one husband. Moreover they form a special group in the church (I Timothy 5.14).

Another demand for fidelity and unity lived out in a Christian way is the obligation to break with an adulterous or promiscuous partner. Not in order to remarry: there is no question whatsoever of divorce. But if a spouse lives in a situation which is seen to be immoral, it is no longer possible for one who wants to live a Christian life to be united with him or her, at least to come to terms with the sexual practices which are censured, because they disrupt the profound unity of the married couple. In these conditions, to maintain a physical union bereft of its spiritual dimension becomes a form of debauchery. Thus true fidelity lived out in faith can demand what nowadays we would call a physical separation.

However, the first theologians were aware that that is often difficult, and that alongside the demand for purity and witness in a church which seeks to escape the perversity of the world, there is also a call for mercy and forgiveness.

A profound sense of the grace of God

This way of looking at things might seem to us to be very 'purist'. Whereas the first Christians set out to mark themselves off from a universe which was thought to be rushing to perdition, we live in a world in which we have a different awareness of the relationship between believers and non-believers and of the perpetual mixture of good and evil. That is why no one nowadays would dream of reviving all the rigour of the ancient discipline of the church. But it is still necessary to see the profound significance of this discipline, which the present-day church continues to defend in other forms.

In the name of the irreversible commitment of God to humanity, the primitive church denounced the temptation to consider the fidelity of the married couple only in terms of the advantage that either partner saw in it. Thus in fact it already put in question both a 'contract' conceived of in the form of a system of assurance that could always be revoked, and 'trial marriage', another form of assurance, this time a preventive one. However, there was no need to legislate in this sphere: trust in the grace of God which was experienced in the community was enough for accepting and living out the Christian demand in a positive way.

Marriage in St Augustine's perspective

In the fourth century, the church, which had now become 'official' appeared more and more as a religious organization for the masses. So we are necessarily a long way away from the first communities who stood out from the pagan world by the purity of small groups which were ready to commit themselves deeply for their faith. It was at this time that Augustine, bishop and famous theologian, described the church as the net in which good and bad fish were mixed. The 'purism' of the first days had disappeared.

The Bishop of Hippo had been brought up in a 'mixed' family, which in concrete terms meant a conflicting education: his father, a pagan, was delighted at his first sexual adventures, while his mother Monica, a Christian, was disturbed by them.

The young Augustine, who was an unbeliever, led a life which he later condemned as dissolute, though it was in complete conformity to the morals of the time. When a student, he had a mistress who bore him a son. His conversion marked the break with his former way of life, which he saw as an obstacle to encounter with God.

However, alongside paganism with a very free morality, the age was marked by currents of thought which played down physical and sexual reality: Manichaeism, which contrasted a material world created by an evil God with an ethereal world, to which the God of light called humanity; and Neoplatonism, exalting an intellectual life detached from earthly chances. Perhaps because he had strong guilt-feelings, Augustine had for a while been tempted by the former doctrine, but he soon departed from it once he saw its profound contradictions. On the other hand, as a convert, it was in the direction of Neoplatonism that he sought to work out his Christianity. That

Fifteenth-century miniature. *Photo J.-L. Charmet*

explains why the theology of this great Western Christian thinker failed to recognize the value of married life, which in his eyes was marred by sexual passion and pleasure.

However, Augustine had to recognize the legitimacy of marriage. He then developed a theory showing that matrimonial union, though polluted by physical desire, finds a value in submitting itself to a superior end: procreation.

This doctrine was to have profound repercussions right down the history of Christian spirituality. Pressed to extremes, it ended up in Jansenism, which could envisage sexual life only in terms of 'conjugal duty'. But it also explains what is called catholic 'natalism': marriage is endorsed only in terms of children, and the life of the married couple is forgotten.

People are aware nowadays of the serious difficulties which this pessimistic view of sexual life entails. Modern thought, by giving the body its due, and stressing the way in which marriage allows a real spiritual relationship, has led the church to compensate for a former view of marriage which was linked to a certain type of thought bound up with a limited historical situation.

That does not mean that we have to reject the whole Augustinian theology of marriage. Augustine saw very clearly the danger of a sexual life centred on the quest for pleasure for its own sake, and consequently of the risk which people constantly face: being cut off from every spiritual dimension of the conjugal relationship and every opening on transcendence, on God. By continuing to recall the significance of a morality of marriage which leads to children, the church opposes the disappearance of the generosity of love. It affirms that if a married couple systematically exclude children they will kill off the roots of that which can bring them life: they condemn themselves to spiritual barrenness as well as physical barrenness. They cut themselves off from the realm of freedom and trust in God.

Ecclesiastical authority takes charge of the commitment to marriage

In the course of the later Middle Ages, the weakening of civil power led the church authorities steadily to take over social control of matrimonial unions. However, for all that, a formal

Clandestine marriages and secret marriages

'Eating, drinking, sleeping together, that seems to me to be marriage, but the church must approve it.'

The first part of this old adage from the sixteenth century gives a good indication of the matter-of-fact way in which people originally regarded marriage. Living together was a way of affirming that one was married. It was what was known as marriage by consent (by the agreement of the two parties). It is the reality that we find in a number of extra-matrimonial situations today.

But this form of union was taken very seriously. This was not simply a 'free union' which could be broken up at will. But there was a risk of that happening if the couple, having been involved privately in marriage, did not make it official. Hence the mistrust of 'clandestine marriage' and, in 1215, the regulation imposed on the faithful at the Lateran Council that they should go through certain formalities (the publication of banns, and a nuptial blessing by the clergy). But for all that, the church did not make the validity of marriage conditional on any of these forms. Clandestine marriage could not be allowed. But it was nevertheless valid and could not be dissolved.

So the proof of such marriages could only come from the oath made by the parties or the actual situation confirmed by evidence: 'If a man has kept and fed publicly in his house a woman as a wife and has had relations with her . . .' The reality of the union suggested marriage by consent.

But this presumption could still be rejected. So there had to be 'proofs'.

'You have to have the church.' Subsequently the state would say, 'You have to have the registry office.' A new development from the Council of Trent (sixteenth century, and from the end of the eighteenth century for civil marriage) was that simple union by consent was no longer allowed because it gave rise to insoluble problems.

Clandestine marriage must not be confused with secret marriage, i.e. a marriage contracted before valid witnesses which is not made public for a variety of social reasons.

commitment entered into before clergy was not regarded as a religious reality. Subsequently, when reflection developed on this, there were even long discussions as to whether this public commitment was bound up with Christian marriage. Many thought it necessary to protect marriage with the formalism of a ceremony: the spiritual value of marriage (what was later to be called its sacramental grace) derives in the first place from the continuing union of the couple, of which the public commitment is only the starting point. This position leads to the awareness that it is the couple who confer marriage on themselves throughout their lives and that this derives from them, not from the priest.

In the twelfth century, Pope Alexander III recognized the formal 'I do' of the commitment made before the representative of the church as the basic act of Christian union. He certainly continued to affirm that the effective and lasting

Mutual Consent Certified, Jean André, end of thirteenth century. *Photo G. Dagli Orti*

bond (including sexual union) between the couple is what makes up marriage. However, the act of commitment is equally an integral part of it, by virtue of the fact that it inaugurates this new situation.

A little later, in 1274, at the Council of Lyons, certain bishops spoke of marriage as a sacrament. So the church sought to develop what remained only an implicit practice.

At the beginning of the Renaissance there was an important shift. The church authorities sought to reserve legal control of the contract to themselves by relating it, as a public commitment defined according to certain rules, to the sacrament. It was therefore affirmed that it is *by their public consent before the church* that the new couple partake in divine grace. Consequently the sacramental celebration and the formality of the

---

A quite separate sacrament

'So what grace does the sacrament of marriage confer?'

'It is a curb on concupiscence,' replied Peter Lombard in the twelfth century.

'That's rather negative,' says the idealist.

'But it's not too bad,' retorts the realist in an informed way.

'There's a much better way,' says Thomas Aquinas (died 1274), a century later: 'Marriage confers the grace that it symbolizes, i.e. the love which united Christ and the church, the love with which Christ died for his church' (cf. Ephesians 5.25ff.).

From then on the sacrament has not been the moment when the couple exchange the words 'I do': it has all the dullness, all the tedium of married people living together. 'Marriage is not the consent itself but the shared life and shared plans which begin with the consent. Strictly speaking the consent is not the sign of the union of Christ and the church but only of the decision, in Christ, to be united with the church.' The sacrament is the 'conjugal and family partnership', the 'partnership of love' of which Vatican II speaks in *Gaudium et Spes*, 47.1, the loving community, visible and fashioned as an everyday sign for humankind.

T. Rey-Mermet, *Ce que Dieu a uni*, 1974

In feudal society

The key to the aristocratic system of values was probably what twelfth-century Latin texts referred to as *probitas*, a valour of body and soul that produced both prowess and magnanimity. In those days everyone thought this supreme quality was transmitted through the blood. The function of marriage was to ensure that the manly virtue of valour was passed on in honour from one generation to the next, that blood was propagated in such a way that it did not, as they said then, degenerate, i.e., lose its genetic virtues. The purpose of marriage was to unite a valiant progenitor to a wife in such a manner that his legitimate son, bearer of the blood and name of a valourous ancestor, should be able to bring that ancestor to life again in his own person. But all depended on the wife. She was not regarded as a mere passive terrain, as she is even today in some black African cultures. In Carolingian and post-Carolingian Europe people believed that women produced sperm, or at least that both the man and the woman contributed to the act of conception, and that the immediate effect of sexual intercourse was to mingle indissolubly the blood of the two partners.

Georges Duby, *The Knight, the Lady and the Priest*, tr. Barbara Bray, Pantheon Books 1983 and Penguin Books 1984, p. 37.

commitment before the appropriate legal authority were made identical. The priest then began to play an essential role in marriage.

By virtue of the mentality inherited from a warrior society, and as a continuation of Roman law, the Christian lawyers surrounded marriage with a very complex system of prohibitions: this explains the numerous declarations of nullity in royal marriages in that period.

Marriage defined as a sacrament

In the middle of the sixteenth century, reacting against the identification of sacrament with contract, Luther declared that the marital union derives from natural law bound up with creation: the church is not the creator of true marriage; one can live out marriage without finding oneself bound up with Christ; marriage is not to be put on the same level as sacraments like baptism and eucharist, willed by Christ to commit believers to follow him, since marital union is not intrinsically bound up with faith. Without denying that marriage can be lived out in Christian terms, Luther denies it the quality of a sacrament. The church cannot do more than bless a union which is contracted independently of it.

By contrast, defining the sacraments in a different way from Luther, the Council of Trent (1545–1563) affirmed that the natural reality of the marital union takes on a new dignity by virtue of its religious consecration.

In defining marriage as a sacrament, the Council of Trent was not reflecting on the way in which marital union draws the couple into the current of the life of Christ. It was simply saying: Jesus has given a new meaning to this union and has made it the source of grace. *The church is responsible for this significance and for the communication of this grace. That is why it defends its right to speak on the matter.*

In fact the Council of Trent is not too concerned to specify how marriage fits into the current of the life of Christ. Having affirmed this fact, it is concerned above all to provide a canonical (legal) definition of the conditions under which the church recognizes marriage as having true sacramental value.

This is an important gain, since it allows a reaction against what was a real plague in previous ages: clandestine marriages which in fact were simply unions made and unmade as the couple willed, scorning the essential demands of true love. But this gain brought with it a loss. For it led to a stress on the public and therefore legal character of marriage. Christians were now led to consider 'going before the parson' as the only Christian reality which counted. They forgot that the true sign of the spiritual reality, that through which there is effective participation in divine grace, is effective communal life. In its profound reality Christian marriage, instituted in the presence of the community, is celebrated anew each day in the act of fidelity and the giving and receiving on the part of the couple.

What is a sacrament?

The church has always had recourse to the idea of sacraments, but without initially feeling the need to define their nature: all the realities of existence were seen as being embraced in the new life engendered by faith in Christ. Some actions continued to be performed in accordance with the gospel without any attempt being made to classify them or to define them. It was St Augustine's view that every sacrament is 'the sign of a sacred reality', 'the visible sign of an invisible grace'. But in this perspective everything can become a sacrament: by evoking faith a simple image, an icon, or a grace which gives a Christian character to a meal can be declared to be a sacrament. In fact in the eleventh century Peter Damian, bishop and 'doctor' of the church (and therefore a recognized scholar) declared that there were twelve sacraments.

But in the following century an unknown author put forward an idea which illuminated what in Augustine had only been implicit: a sacrament is an *effective* symbol, a sign which confers the grace that it symbolizes. So it is that the sacraments of the church have come to be identified as being *seven* in number.

Modern linguistic philosophers have reflected on what can constitute *efficacious* words. A contract, a promise, is not just a set of words. It creates a new situation, it *acts*. In order for there to be a sacrament there must be something more: the sign (word, action) must correspond to the will of Christ and constitute a form of commitment to discipleship. If it corresponds to these conditions, this sign creates something new. It is drawn into the current of life which flows from Jesus: it comes to participate in 'grace'.

At the source of contemporary difficulties

If the definition of marriage as a sacrament is put in the continuing tradition of the church's experience, the conditions in which it was thought of can only raise grave difficulties. In a bourgeois society which is increasingly marked by the development of the economy and therefore little concerned for individuals and their freedom, do we not end up with a sacralization of a social contract which excludes any real encounter? Though that need not prove fatal, it involves considerable risks, and we know the dramas it leads to.

The danger of the identification of marriage with a social contract is all the greater when the bond between the Catholic church and a society defined *a priori* as Christian has made the marriage blessing in social terms an obligatory point of transition for those who have been baptized, no matter what their faith may in fact be. In that case we end up with a paradox: in a society in which nominal Christians are no longer always believers, the church recognizes the validity of a marriage only if it is sacramental. But at the same time it must be remembered that the sacrament is only valid through faith.

Here we have the source of contemporary

A marriage of a social kind

Under the old order the 'organizing idea' of marriage, one might say its aim, was indisputably of a social kind. By marriage, a man or a woman entered into a new 'state', acquired a status which had been defined by society and even more important, for society . . . The status of the partners, their specific reciprocal rights and duties, the laws and customs relating to the legitimacy of children, the conditions of inheritance, all and everything was governed by this priority of the social dimension.

This priority did not mean that the individual derived no advantage from the institution. In fact he existed as a legal entity only by virtue of his membership of the family, which gave him his identity and his status . . . Marriage was the act *par excellence* by which he became a recognized member of society: it alone was the basis for the legitimacy of his children, it alone governed his relationships and determined the social space in which he had to live and work. So one can understand how the social characteristics of a family unit were largely determined by its situation in society. Among those with property, a concern to keep the family inheritance intact determined family attitudes and behaviour. This preoccupation was especially a factor in matrimonial strategy. In this type of family, marriage was the best way of consolidating or increasing family property. The question of succession generally left little room for decisions or arrangements. By contrast marriage and family alliance, which involved determining endowments, were the prime instruments of matrimonial politics.

So how can it be thought scandalous that the choice of partner was the business of the head of the family? The logic of the system could only leave so serious a decision to the one who was

Divorce, Lesueur. *Gouache*. Musée Carnavalet. *Photo J.-L. Charmet*

responsible for the family heritage. And how could one regard as unjust the rights of the firstborn, which were simply an indication of the imperative need to keep this heritage intact. The fact that some of the younger members of the family would probably never get married was the price paid to ensure the integrity and continuity of the 'house'.

The imperative need to 'hand down' the family heritage reinforced the cultural solidarity between the family and society as a whole, where that solidarity existed. A concern to perpetuate the family heritage could not exist outside a concern for the stability of an organization and a culture, which gave its significance and dignity to the name of the house. The family could defend its heritage only by showing solidarity, at least in principle, with the political and economic situation which allowed its stability, its reproduction and its growth.

L. Roussel, *Le Mariage dans la societé française*

They were in love because they were married . . .

Not every family had a family inheritance. Not every farmer owned his land, and those who did could not settle all their sons on it. For the poor, whether they lived in the town or in the country, the idea of handing on an inheritance hardly made sense. The way they acted was governed by a concern to survive; the choice of a spouse was determined by the mechanisms of affinity and homogamy; and the distribution of tasks within the family was imposed by the constraints of their profession. There was probably more freedom within the make-up of these families, as in their way of life; more room for manoeuvre than in families which had an ancestral heritage. In particular, the choice of a partner did not follow a family strategy: mutual attraction had a role here.

Generally speaking, it is probably a caricature of reality, or at least a simplification of it, to claim that there was no place for sentiment in those families which had an ancestral estate. How could we think that marriage did not have a deep and stabilizing social effect on those involved in it? Sentiment was indeed there, sometimes deep and lasting. But it was to some degree controlled by the obvious fact that the marriage bond meant more than subjective satisfaction. In sum, it all seemed as though individual emotions were thought to be determined by collective norms. One might be tempted to say that people were in love because they were married rather than that they married because they were in love. Again, it is necessary to put the word 'love' in quotation marks, since it probably denoted very different feelings from those which we understand by the term today.

L. Roussel, *Le Mariage dans la societé française*

---

difficulties. Priests find themselves torn between a legal demand which normally leads them to bless in church the marriage of all those baptized persons who ask for it and a pastoral sense which moves them to confer the sacrament only on those who want really to live out their union in the perspective of Christian faith. For their part, nominal Christians too often fail to understand the true meaning of the sacrament, since they have reduced Christian marriage to formal commitment made in church.

Even more seriously, marriage tends to become an act performed by individuals who are cut off from all real Christian fellowship which represents a way of life that stands out from that of the world around. The couple no longer has the environment of this 'new family' which Christ meant to bring into being, a church which could allow the couple really to bring their married life in line with the kingdom of God which is already present in this world.

In such conditions it is not surprising that Christian marriage, too often devoid of its authentic significance, is put in question by new generations, sometimes even by young people living in the faith.

So is it necessary to reject as purely negative all doctrinal and legal reflection by the church on the sacrament? Surely not. For it marks an awareness that coherent love exists only where it expresses itself by making a public statement. A love which does not present itself to others does not shine out and cannot attain its true dimensions. In this sense the church rejects all those who shut themselves up in their own private world and affirm that society has no place in their union. The couple cannot live without interfering with society; the Christian family cannot blossom as such without a relationship with the community of faith. But this interference is truly possible only where there is a precise and definite language, recognized by all, which consequently leads to clear relationships. And it is no coincidence if one feels ill at ease with a couple who do not say clearly what their relationship is, who do not state their plans, because they reject or fail to recognize the social language of the marriage rite. If this rite is absent, that is to say, if there is no expression which can be clearly understood by all, this couple cannot be surprised at not being recognized.

Finally, the problem of the legitimacy of the conjugal union is not the expression of a fear of sexuality which is not channeled through the law, as so many people think. It is above all the expression of a demand for the *truth* of love.

The church and civil marriage

To begin with, the church knew no celebration of marriage other than 'civil' marriage. However, from the moment that it became fully aware of the need to link the married life of Christians with their faith it claimed the right to celebrate the marriages of believers. This led it to devalue a commitment of a purely secular kind: in fact the introduction of civil marriage, which came about after a period of Christianity during which the church had complete control over the laws of marriage, often took place as a reaction against it, and out of a concern to deny the church all rights in the matter, even over believers.

The situation has changed today. Even if in theory, where the baptized are involved, ecclesiastical law continues to recognize as valid only those marriages which have been celebrated according to its rules, the church has been led to reaffirm the value of civil marriage for those who are not its members. It also accepts that in fact a number of those who have been baptized but no longer believe make an authentic act of commitment by having a civil marriage. It is necessary to go even further and recognize that civil marriage contracted by believers is already a real commitment on the secular level, even if this commitment only takes on a really Christian dimension as a result of marriage in church.

In 1980, during an important meeting of bishops in Rome, Pope John-Paul II acknowledged the value of the life of those who have only undergone a civil marriage.

5
Marriage and Canon Law

Canon law ('canon' = rule) is the term applied to all the rules which determine the disciplinary function of the church.

In respect of marriage, this law tells us the conditions under which the authority of the Catholic church recognizes marriage as authentic (its validity) and what it believes that the character of marriage should be. So it defines the essentials for real accord: the consent of the partners to become a couple, and the recognition of this by the community.

Canon law seeks to show the character of a practical response to the call of Christ. This is a matter of embodying the love of God in the marriage union, taking account of the value that a given society sees in it. So canon law takes into account both an absolute fact and the perception of marriage that people have in different cultures. Depending on the time and place, the church has sought to evangelize particular aspects of marital union which changing awareness has brought into view. Similarly, it regulates in different ways the manner in which marriage is celebrated depending on existing customs.

The fundamental nature of marriage

Canon 1055 – 1. The matrimonial covenant, by which a man and a woman establish between themselves a partnership of the whole of life, is by its nature ordered towards the good of the spouses and the procreation and education of offspring; this covenant between baptized persons has been raised by Christ the Lord to the dignity of a sacrament.

2. For this reason a matrimonial contract cannot validly exist between baptized persons unless it is also a sacrament by that fact.

Canon 1056 – The essential properties of marriage are unity and indissolubility, which in Christian marriage obtain a special firmness in virtue of the sacrament.

Canon 1057. – 1. Marriage is brought about through the consent of the parties, legitimately manifested between persons who are capable according to law of giving consent; no human power can replace this consent.

2. Matrimonial consent is an act of the will by which a man and a woman, through an irrevocable covenant, mutually give and accept each other in order to establish marriage.

Pastoral care and what must precede celebration of marriage

Canon 1063 – Pastors of souls are obliged to see to it that their own ecclesial community furnishes the Christian faithful assistance so that the matrimonial state is maintained in a Christian spirit and makes progress towards perfection. This assistance is especially to be furnished through:

1. preaching, catechesis adapted to minors, youths and adults, and even the use of the media of social communications so that through these means the Christian faithful may be instructed concerning the meaning of Christian marriage and the duty of Christian spouses and parents;

2. personal preparation for entering marriage so that through such preparation the parties may be predisposed towards the holiness and duties of their new state;

3. a fruitful liturgical celebration of marriage clarifying that the spouses signify and share in that mystery of unity and of fruitful love that exists between Christ and the Church;

4. assistance furnished to those already married so that, while faithfully maintaining and protecting the conjugal covenant, they may day by day come to lead holier and fuller lives in their families.

Family tree of
a couple.
Decretals of
Gratian,
fourteenth
century
miniature.
Photo B N

Matrimonial consent

Canon 1095 – They are incapable of contracting marriage:
  1. who lack the sufficient use of reason;
  2. who suffer from grave lack of discretion of judgment concerning essential matrimonial rights and duties which are to be mutually given and accepted;
  3. who are not capable of assuming the essential obligations of matrimony due to causes of a psychic nature.

All quotations from the 1983 Code of Canon Law are taken from *The Code of Canon Law. A Text and Commentary commissioned by the Canon Law Society of America*, ed. James A. Coriden, Thomas J. Green and Donald E. Heintschel, Geoffrey Chapman and Paulist Press 1985.

Without going into all the details here, I shall quote some essential articles from the new regulations in the Code of Canon Law promulgated in 1983. Michel Legrain, Professor of Canon Law at the Catholic Institute in Paris, has made some comments on them.

Question to Fr Legrain: What changes do you think that the present code makes to the view of marriage in the Catholic church?

Answer: The very conception of marriage has been changed in comparison with the past. From the first canon on, the tone is different. Where in 1917 canon law spoke of a contract, the new code now talks of a covenant. True, it was formerly said this this contract had the dignity of a sacrament, but all the same it remained a contract, and it was governed by contractual legislation. Thinking in terms of a covenant has the advantage of being both more biblical and more compatible both with our own Western mentality and with the marriage customs of so-called primitive peoples.

In the contractual perspective it is enough that two 'fit' persons (in the canonical sense of the term) should know and ratify the essentials of the contract: once possession has been taken of the object of the contract, in other words, after sexual intercourse, the contract is irrevocable, even if in human terms this union is one of radical poverty or degrading violence. According to the strange expression which became customary, the marriage is said to be 'consummated', since the agreement of wills leads to a physiological act. This is a terrible impoverishment of personal union.

With Vatican II and the 1983 code, marriage is seen as a 'profound communion of life and love'. In order to bring this about it is no longer enough to be capable of expressing one's intent. It is necessary to have what is needed for this communion to grow and last: a certain emotional capacity and a psychological and spiritual aptitude on the part of the couple for complete commitment. This personal gift goes far beyond the simple possibility of genital activity with a view to procreation. In this perspective 'consummation' is no longer just a physical act. It must come about in a human way, says canon 1061; and nowadays we often find church tribunals declaring null marriages which have been followed by full sexual intercourse and even by the procreation of one or two children.

Question: So is marriage no longer regarded above all in terms of procreation?

Answer: In effect, yes. The 1917 code said, 'The primary end of marriage is the procreation and education of children; the secondary end is mutual help and the allaying of concupiscence' (Canon 1013, 1). Despite the demand of many Christians who wanted to see 'conjugal' put before 'parental', Pius XII continued to affirm the subordination of the first end of marriage to the second (*Address to the Midwives*, 29 October 1951). But in discussing conjugal union Vatican II mentions mutual support before fertility (*Gaudium et Spes* 48, *Lumen Gentium* 11). Along these lines our code (1055, 1) explains that the fellowship of married life is by its very nature ordained for the good of the spouses and for parental fertility. So there is no longer stress on one dimension at the expense of the other: they are partners, each playing a different role, depending on the stage that the life of the couple has reached.

Question: So, as compared with the old law, which was above all centred on the institution in a concern to assure the continuity of the human species, does the new code seem to pay more attention to individuals?

Answer: Yes, to a certain degree, but only to a certain degree. In fact the Latin church found itself torn between a desire to serve the common good and a desire to serve that of individuals. How could one avoid sacrificing individuals for the institution? But how could one safeguard the indispensable constraint exercised by the institution in the face of individual whims and desires? The new code seeks to avoid constraint and the limitation of freedom whenever these are not indispensable. Does it succeed completely? It is striking that it is more concerned to preserve the institution of matrimony than to occupy itself with the misfortunes of certain couples. Canon 1060 quotes in its entirety the old text which stipulates that when there is any persistent doubt about the validity of a marriage, the presumption must be in favour of marriage, and not in favour of personal freedom. The local ecclesiastical tribunal could have been given the right to evaluate the situation. Note also the pre-eminence given to the defence of the marriage bond from processes affecting the validity of a marriage, and the modesty of the role given to the advocacy of individual freedom. One cannot but regret the slowness of the procedure in such processes.

Question: Is there not a lack of concern for individuals in section 2 of canon 1055 which states that any contract between baptized persons is also a sacrament? So does the fact of being baptized suppress the right to just a 'natural' marriage, if husband and wife, as non-believers or semi-believers, are strangers to the idea of the sacrament?

Answer: There is in fact a great problem here. According to the code, two baptized people cannot really be married unless they are married sacramentally. So contemporary legislation does not take account of whether married couples believe or not. If both parties are baptized, it takes this situation as a basis for decreeing that their conjugal bond must be a sacramental one. Even the neglect of or scorn for the sacramental aspect of marriage on the part of an unbelieving couple does not do away with this religious character. If that were really excluded, the code says, there would be no marriage.

Nowadays in our Western countries a great many of those who have been baptized but are either indifferent to the Christian faith or blatant unbelievers continue to get married in church. So their marriage bond is regarded as being a sacramental one. All they wanted was a quiet little ceremony and they find themselves saddled with the responsibility of signifying the love of Christ for the church. This compulsory condition gravely disfigures the sacrament.

It must be recognized that it is difficult to understand how a baby baptized a Catholic but then brought up outside the faith can be subjected twenty years later to this canonical limitation of his or her natural right to marriage to the point when, from a religious perspective, he or she has no other choice than to accept the sacrament or cohabit. Even supposing that such a person is not bothered about canon law, the problem remains, for part of public opinion influenced by the doctrine of the church does not consider anyone who was not married in church to be really married.

So we can only hope for official recognition of the legitimacy of civil marriage for a couple who want to express their union socially in conformity with their present state of unbelief or semi-belief.

Question: How do you explain the unsuitability of this legislation?

Answer: History shows variations in church control over the marriage of Christians down the ages. The very close connection between marriage and sacrament is bound up with a context in which there was a clash between church and states and in which the church thought that it would do those who were baptized a service by linking contract and sacrament. However, in present circumstances this identification generally does more harm than good. Until there has been theological clarification in this sphere, our attempts at pastoral *aggiornamento* over matrimony will remain ambiguous.

Question: So as far as you are concerned, the law should vary depending on social and cultural situations?

Answer: Yes. There are societies or periods of history in which the human reality of marriage is lived out in a context which stresses its social, legal and canonical aspects. At other times the personal aspect and the commitment implied by the marital union stand out more clearly. By imposing on attitudes characteristic of one particular culture a pattern of legislation conceived on the basis of an overall view which is alien to that culture, one ends up with a disaster, or at least legislation which does not fit. That is the risk that the Latin church runs if it ceases to adapt its law to the diversity of situations that we know today. This calls for legislation which is much more flexible, or even varies depending on the cultural background. The law must always be at the service of the evangelization of society, and to that end it must take account of the particular values of a society.

6

The Sacrament of Marriage Today

It is now possible to understand better what the church is saying when it speaks of marriage as a sacrament.

A new way of living out love

The history that we have just traced helps us to understand the mistake made by those who interpret Christian marriage in terms of a legal contract. Marriage certainly contains this aspect, to the degree that mutual commitment in marriage is expressed by means of a social language. But that is only the superficial appearance of the essence of marriage, which is to live out love as Christ lived it. This essence should explode from within the legalistic and commercial mentality which threatens true love and condemns it to perdition.

At the same time we can also see the mistake of the anti-legalist reaction which, on the pretext of rediscovering the spontaneity of love, fails to understand the need to integrate it into a wider perspective which gives it an ultimate meaning and saves it. If it is thought of as a reality which is utterly self-sufficient, sooner or later this love can only end up in failure, even if that failure is simply that of the death of the beloved.

The true sacrament of marriage is the sign of a call coming from Jesus Christ inviting husband and wife to let themselves be caught up into the current of his grace and thus at the heart of married life to embody the renewed life that he raises up in us. It is set in motion when husband and wife ratify the vocation of all human beings to follow the way marked out by Jesus. It is an act of trust in God which affirms that through joy and pain, success or failure, the spontaneous attraction of man to woman and woman to man is transformed into true charity, into a charity which takes on the value of eternity. The sacrament shows how this love, as strong as death, cannot be extinguished, for its features are features of fire, a flame of the Lord (Song of Songs 8.6).

Understood in this way, the sacrament of marriage has a place in the extension of the basic sacraments of Christian life: it calls for a practical response to baptismal vocation at the heart of a particularly important situation; it is a call to put into a physical, emotional and spiritual form the communion with God and the neighbour which is brought about mysteriously and in fullness in the eucharist. It feeds on the gift of the Spirit and offers a window on it. There is even a need to stress its relationship to the sacrament of penance, to the degree that the family, the place not only of encounter, but also of confrontation, conflict and failure, is at the same time that of the reconciliation to which a specific sacrament of the church invites us. So it is a crossroads of Christian life in its totality.

Human love, Christian love: eros and agape

What kind is our love?

In his eighth homily on the First Epistle of St John, commenting on the apostle's insistence that we should 'love one another', St Augustine writes:

We ought not to love people in the same way in which we hear gluttons say, I love thrushes.

You may ask, why does he love them?

It is so that he may kill, that he may consume. He says he loves, and to this end he loves them, that they may cease to be; to this end he loves them, that he may make away with them. What-ever we love in the way of food, to this end we love it, that it may be destroyed and we refreshed. Are we to love people so as to destroy them?

But there is a certain friendliness of well-wishing, by which we desire at some time or other to do good to those whom we love. And if there is no good that we can do, the benevolence, the wishing well, is itself enough for the one who loves.

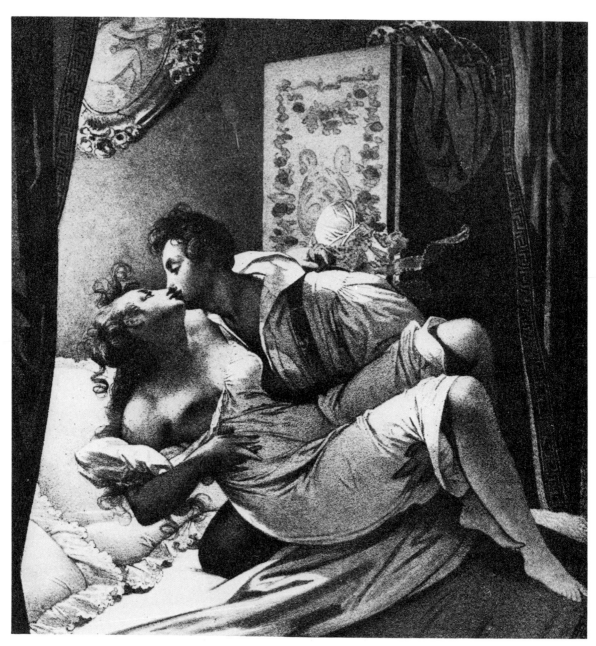

The Alcove of Romantic Love. Etching by Maurin, 1799–1850. *Photo Edimedia*

The English term love is extremely ambiguous, because it can signify very different, if not opposed realities: sexuality, even in its most brutal or commercial form, both outside marriage and in some marriage contracts, and the divine reality in which the Creator has his creature participate. The Greek language is richer in this respect: there is *eros* which denotes the spontaneous reality of human love, but there is also *agape* – a term specific to the Bible – which denotes the prevenient love of God for humanity (it is the original significance of the word charity).

The distinction between the love of desire and divine love, between eros and agape, is of vital importance. However, it should not be transformed into an absolute separation, far less an opposition. So it is important to specify the relationship which exists between these two orders of reality: for the Christian good news about love consists finally in a call to unite them.

The value of the love of man and woman

It is important to affirm the immense value of eros, of love, in its most secular dimensions. A reality willed by God, it is and always remains a sign of him, the language which allows us to approach him, to be like him.[1] The simple fact that a man and a woman discover their radical physical, emotional, cultural and spiritual inadequacy through the perception of the *other* partner of itself already counteracts the sinful tendency to delight in oneself.[2] The other person's need obliges one to recognize one's limits even if, through certain forms of sexual relationships, there may be an attempt to recover one's proud solitude over against the other. Eros provokes the human being to discover that he or she can only live fully thanks to another, and in so doing

Clay sarcophagus from Cerveteri. Villa Giula, Rome

shows some people what the Wholly Other can be. A non-believer can experience that just as much as a believer.

So it has to be said that eros, as experienced by any human being, can imply a real transcendence of simple desire and be a window on the divine transcendence, even when the latter is not expressly recognized. It can involve a profound fidelity, a call, a secret invocation, the infinite dimension of which does not necessarily appear in all its clarity to the person who has this experience, but which is nevertheless one of its moving forces.

The person who, in love, sees this opening towards the other, finds access to a world of communication the origin of which the Christian affirms to be God himself. Through eros, agape can unfold. By living out an authentic love in its fullness, human beings are already reborn of God, even if they do not clearly recognize this fact. They affirm the reality by their very love. Thus Christ could tell a woman who was a public sinner that she was saved because she had loved much.

But secular love, eros, leads to agape only if it is truly transformed and converted within. It has to give up keeping its riches to itself, and agree to be in some way received, given, the fruit of grace.

69

Love comes from God

Beloved,
let us love one another;
for love is of God,
and he who loves
is born of God
and knows God.
He who does not love
does not know God;
for God is love.

In this the love of God was made manifest
among us,
that God sent his only Son into the world,
so that we might live through him.
In this is love, not that we loved God
but that he loved us
and sent his Son
to be the expiation for our sins.

Beloved,
if God so loved us,
we ought also to love one another.
No man has ever seen God;
if we love one another,
God abides in us and his love is perfected in us.

I John 4.7–12

Why go to confession before marriage?

It is a unique adventure, an enormous risk, a success as difficult as a home. Two sinners share their lives and seek to unite the beating of their hearts. Does one leave them to commit themselves and play this dangerous game without being assured that they have been given redemptive grace and that within their intimacy, in the service of their struggle towards goodness and the light, they have taken God as their confidant and support? *The church refuses to be responsible for any other union.* No purely human love can ensure that two lives come together until the last evening, with a matching sparkle, given that love is frivolous, blind, unsatisfied. The divine forgiveness must come down on these hearts where sin dwells.

Moreover, since reconciliation with the Creator is not just an agreement which wins us his good will but a grace which grants us a share in his intimate life, it is necessary for the very love of God to enter into these hearts. Yes, these two beings, whose happiness evil could kill, must love with a heart of flesh in which there beats the heart of God.

A.-M. Carré, *Compagnons d'éternité*, Le Cerf

Agape does not solve all the problems of eros

Christian faith brings no guarantee of temporal success in married life. It does not offer any reflections on sexual methods which guarantee sexual or emotional fulfilment, nor any psycho-logy which makes it possible to avoid conflicts within marriage. On this point the husband and wife are reminded of their own responsibility, that is to say their reflection and their judgment. In certain conditions, a number of marriages come to grief. The loftiest spirituality will not make any difference. Indeed, it can even become dangerous to the degree that it allows the belief that there is no need to think about the specific problems posed by everyday life which are a matter of human thought and common sense.

So it is necessary to consider what can be and what must be the elements of a successful marriage at the level of eros. It is also necessary to plan some teaching leading, sooner or later, to a marriage which has some chance of being more than a lottery. On these points the church can only offer a reminder of natural facts which have been analysed out of secular considerations; in other words, it can refer to good 'marriage counsellors'.

Agape saves eros

By suggesting a reorientation of the impulses of eros, agape fills it with a new dynamism which comes to save it.

As a factor bound up with physical desire, with the call of the senses, eros remains extremely fragile. Finding its own laws only in itself, it is incapable of surmounting certain difficulties. Confronted with illness, madness, neurosis, aging, eros finds it 'quite natural' to renounce fidelity, married unity.

But agape introduces another perspective on love: that of the free gift to the other in response to the free gift of God in Jesus Christ.

Because the believer knows himself or herself to be loved by God, he or she becomes capable of radiating whatever gives him or her life, without expecting anything in return except the very joy of living in love.

I have mentioned the need to think rationally about certain psychological or physiological problems of married life. But the best decisions in this sphere do not get as far as the fundamental question: can love go as far as renouncing out of love for the other any advantage over

Cartoon by Jacques Faizant, from J. Faizant and J. Loew, *Paraboles et Fariboles*, Editions Fayard

him or her that one might expect to hold? Is it capable of rising above the transactional view that I analysed in the first chapter?

It is at this point that one can discover all the riches of an appeal to God in a sacramental celebration which takes place in prayer. For by coming into the presence of God, by appealing to him in this way, a man and a woman open themselves to grace. In so doing they can better grasp the magnitude of what is at stake spiritually in their married life. They can also find new reasons for facing the difficulties in their encounter, and the strength needed to surmount any obstacles.

It is necessary to go even further. Of itself, eros, rich though it may be, necessarily comes up against the supreme obstacle, death. But by faith

71

the believer discovers that this death can be transformed into resurrection. Where the physical and emotional presence disappears, it is possible to find another presence. For love lived in God creates an eternal bond. This is a paradoxical truth which is both crucifying and the source of life: it is sometimes at the very moment when the bond of physical love is loosened that there is a sudden revelation of the possibility of the fullness of the encounter. Anyone who has this experience can discover in the midst of suffering the spiritual reality of a new family, that of the kingdom of God.

Married spirituality

Love, which seeks to be at the heart of marriage, is put in a state of grace on the wedding day. Whereas the sacramental contract immediately comes into force in all its reality, love only begins to give itself to the slow work and the enrichments of charity. It has to learn how to love with the love with which God loves. If this love is faithful, God will use it in what he brings about in the hearts of the married couple, by stripping them of their egotism, by purifying them, teaching them, sometimes roughly, painfully – as in a practical school of sanctity – how to be present to each other in a way which will be in the service of the presence of God. And God will also make use of it through that which cannot be realized in any human love. The appetite for happiness is a window on eternity. Love in a state of grace, love endowed with grace is an introduction to the world of divine life. We know it because we have seen it; love can bring about this miracle of bringing closer and closer together two partners in their love and of increasingly arousing in them hunger and thirst for the God who is love. They are empty and greedy, but the distant ideal of today can become the reality of tomorrow. It is the work of charity.

God is there: he supports and feeds them. God is there, and he leads them to himself.

A.-M. Carré, *Compagnons d'éternité*

Communion in Silent Prayer, Boltraffio. Pinacoteca di Brera, Milan. *Photo Giraudon*

Husband and wife in charge of each other's soul

The attitude of charity is all the more necessary since each partner is responsible for the salvation of the other. Both have charge of the soul. They are joined together the better to participate in the divine life and holiness. Moreover you should not hinder the salvation of the one closest to you but further it, within a disturbed society in which just about everything conspires to make the human individual forget his or her eternal destiny.

In this sense the intimacy of husband and wife participates in that of the Saviour and his church, and the magnificent saying of Father Lacordaire, that the apostle must be the 'particular Christ' for each soul, finds its primary application here. Life is an ascent towards God. By vocation, you have chosen and accepted this being, this complement willed by the Creator, in order the better to rise and to use your own strength to help the rise of another. You are responsible for him or her. You have no right to plead weariness and resort to divorce. And if physical separation is sometimes imposed by painful circumstances, spiritual divorce is condemned for ever. Right to the end, even if it has to be in solitude and after experiencing the most bitter of deceptions, through prayer and penitence you must remain 'the particular Christ' of this being whose betrayal has crucified you.

Only charity can thus achieve the survival of a broken love.

A.-M. Carré, *Compagnons d'éternité*

The Cathedral, Rodin. Stone, 1908. Musée Rodin, Paris. *Photo Bruno Janet*

Prayer is the light of the soul. Ink sketch by Jean Bertholle

The ritual celebration of marriage

Why a marriage service? Is it not an empty formality which kills off spontaneous expression?

It may seem so to those who see things from the outside, as a matter of curiosity. But once couples decide to live together, they instinctively find the need for it. They need to have a way to show others their intentions towards them, for these others in turn to show their intentions towards the new couple. They need to be certain of the basic rules of communication which make up social experience (and being in love is a social experience).

The marriage service consists of a language made up of words and actions. But one does not invent a completely new language; if one did, one would not be understood. One can, however, renew language from within by making use of expressions which are already generally understandable, setting them out to express what one means in an original way.

The church provides a marriage service. This contains a certain number of basic elements. But at the same time the church makes it possible for each couple to organize their own service from the material available within this framework, and indeed to add their own material.

The elements in the church's service are:

1. A time of welcome. It is important to help not only the betrothed but also parents and friends to become aware of what is at stake in this marriage. Together they represent the church.

2. A time for sharing in the Word. By suggesting biblical texts for the celebration the church invites those who are getting married and the congregation to reflect on the significance of marriage, in the light of scripture, and therefore in the Christian perspective. This sharing in the Word can take the form of a dialogue to the degree that the husband and wife show by means of a biblical text which they like how they perceive their commitment.

3. A time of prayer. The church invites the married couple and the congregation to pray and to ask to 'take hold of his grace, to give full rein to love'.

4. The plighting of the troth. This is the essential element in the celebration and takes place in the presence of a priest and witnesses. The civil laws governing marriage vary in different countries. Where a separate civil ceremony is required, as in France and Germany, the formulae used in the religious service can be varied. No set formulae is required in the USA, but in England and Wales all non-established churches must use the wording laid down by the Marriage Act of 1949. If the priest has not been delegated as an authorized person to register marriages under the Act, then a registrar must be present at the service.

5. Tokens of union. The joining of hands and the exchanging of rings are the symbols of fidelity.

The mass, which is not directly part of the rite of marriage but in which believers often embody their commitment, recalls that this commitment is made in the Easter perspective which I stressed all through the reflections on the Bible in earlier chapters.

7

What Kind of Love
will produce the Child?

So far I have hardly mentioned children: formerly, however, they were at the centre of the problem of marriage; so much so, that in society marriage revolved around them: one entered into a legal union in order to have children.

Similarly, we have seen that for a long time in the church some theologians, including the greatest, thought that physical 'concupiscence' could be justified only by subordinating it to the superior good of procreation.

In this perspective the feeling of love which now guides the choice of a partner in marriage was subordinated to a superior imperative. Love came second – and sometimes had no place at all, except to affirm itself outside the bounds of marriage. And when love did come to birth, rooted in the reality of a common life, the impression was that the good of the species, embodied in the child, had by happy chance found support in the blossoming of the relationship between husband and wife.

Does not the modern stress on the married couple amount to a revolution in traditional values, to the point of denying the primacy of the very aim of marriage and subordinating the good of the species to love?

Biologically speaking, love is indeed orientated towards procreation. In the animal kingdom, from which human beings derive one aspect of their being, the sexual organs are above all reproductive organs, and it is only by a stratagem that human beings have finally been able to detach their emotional and physical life from this first imperative, which was the perpetuation of the family and the human species.

At this point we must think a bit more about the direction and possible significance of this change of horizon.

A new way of raising the problem of procreation

A shift in society: from the haphazard child to the wanted child

Human beings have not sought to 'regulate' their reproduction as a result of a will which denies the order of creation. Human reproduction in fact goes beyond the purely natural order which characterizes animal life, which is ruled by instinct. It derives from a 'culture', that is to say from a complex of intentions and means through which a truly human order can come into being.

For to 'give birth' to a child is not just to 'make' it, biologically speaking. It is also to educate it, to bring it to birth in society. And that takes time and effort, above all in an increasingly complex world in which certain spontaneous mechanisms by which individuals used to be integrated into the community no longer work. The more knowledge human beings acquire, the more they become capable of foreseeing and weighing up the future, and the more they seek to organize their family life in terms of what seems to them to be an 'ideal balance', whether personal or social. At the level of the married couple this raises the problem of birth control, just as at the global level of society it raises the problem of 'population control' (which we cannot go into here).

From now on, the discovery of our biological mechanisms has given us real power in this sphere. This is a genuine revolution which has caused a profound upheaval in the mentalities and customs of what are technically the most developed countries. From now on there is a real possibility for children no longer to be produced haphazardly, but as the consequence of a thought-out desire and will.

But at the same time this poses a formidable question: if from now on paternity and maternity can become 'responsible', they must offer a response to a basic question: What is this desire? What is this will?

A shift in the church's view: biological reality, an expression of the spirituality of love

If society's views of children have changed, so too have those of the church, but for different reasons.

In former times sexual intercourse, which was always thought to be suspect, could be justified only by subordinating it to the superior good of having children. But through centuries of experience and trial and error, also spurred on by modern thought on sexuality, the church has dissociated itself from the Manichaean or Neoplatonic conception which had for so long been a burden on its theology of marriage. From now on it can no longer think of the experience of love as simple submission to 'animal concupiscence'; it can see it as a fully human act, involving the body and the spirit, the spiritual through the physical.

This is a real reversal of perspective. For from now on it is no longer the biological fact of reproduction that serves as the justification for the relationship, the spiritual, emotional and physical life, in a word the love, of the couple. The justification for reproduction has to be found in love, which is truly good in itself. The 'primary end of marriage' is no longer the procreation of children, an end towards which emotional relationships and physical satisfaction were entirely ordered, as the old canon law declared. In the new code of the church these three elements are put on the same level: they relate one to the other like three aspects of a single reality of love.

Thus the question posed to the Christian is no longer 'Does the number of your children justify your love life?' but 'Does your love life have such a quality that it bears fruit?'

The question which the church puts to the world is: 'What kind of love will produce the child?'

A child who is desired and wanted . . . But does that not mean a child who is loved? In technologically developed modern societies does the phenomenon of the small family which cherishes either an only child or a number of children carefully planned to suit what are seen to be the conditions in which the family will best flourish meet up with the perspective of the church?

Here, in terms of the child, we return to a question which has already been raised in terms of the love of the husband and wife. Is to desire a child, to want it, to be attached to it, necessarily the same as to love it in the way the gospel uses that word?

We must open the Bible once more, that great mirror of the basic problems of humanity.

Procreation in the biblical perspective

In the Old Testament, it was taken for granted that a couple would have children. Among a people who had not yet arrived at the notion of eternal life, woe to the man who had no descendants! His life lost its meaning. Woe, too, to the barren woman! She was thought to be cursed, since she had not fulfilled her *raison d'être*. So children seemed to be signs of success.

However, some biblical episodes show that reflection rapidly went beyond this immediate view of procreation as a guarantee of the fertility of existence.

The people of God meditate on the sacrifice of Isaac

I have already mentioned Abraham in showing how some episodes in the Genesis story which at first sight are disconcerting and strange in fact raise fundamental problems about marriage. We must now look at the story of the sacrifice of Isaac, better known than the stories which precede it, but no less enigmatic. Its strange, if not repulsive, character forms a real 'test' for human desire.

People have tried their best to rid this story of its scandalous character. For how is it possible to conceive of a God who calls on a man to kill his own child?

The first method consists in reducing the meaning of the text to the facts which perhaps lie at its origin: the story is said to be 'unhistorical'. Its purpose is said to be to explain the name of a place (here 'The Lord will provide') by resorting to an originally Canaanite legend. On taking possession of the country the Hebrews are said to have incorporated this old story into their own history. But they will have expurgated it to some degree. For where the Canaanites in fact sacrificed the firstborn son, God saves Isaac. Thus through what becomes a history of the testing of faith, revelation finally comes to affirm that God does not want the death of the child but his life.

Whatever the value of such an interpretation may be, it is certainly far from taking account of the depth of the text and explaining the reasons why it has become so important in the meditation of the Jewish people, who recognized themselves in Isaac . . . and in the meditation of the

---

God put Abraham to the test

After these things God tested Abraham, and said to him, 'Abraham!' And he said, 'Here am I.' He said, 'Take your son, your only son Isaac, whom you love, and go to the land of Moriah, and offer him there as a burnt offering upon one of the mountains of which I shall tell you.' So Abraham rose early in the morning, saddled his ass, and took two of his young men with him, and his son Isaac; and he cut the wood for the burnt offering, and arose and went to the place of which God had told him. On the third day Abraham lifted up his eyes and saw the place afar off. Then Abraham said to his young men, 'Stay here with the ass; I and the lad will go yonder and worship, and come again to you.' And Abraham took the wood of the burnt offering, and laid it on Isaac his son; and he took in his hand the fire and the knife. So they went both of them together. And Isaac said to his father Abraham, 'My father!' And he said. 'Here am I, my son.' He said, 'Behold, the fire and the wood; but where is the lamb for a burnt offering?' Abraham said, 'God will provide himself the lamb for a burnt offering, my son.' So they went both of them together.

When they came to the place of which God had told him, Abraham built an altar there, and laid the wood in order, and bound Isaac his son, and laid him on the altar, upon the wood. Then Abraham put forth his hand, and took the knife to slay his son. But the angel of the Lord called to him from heaven, and said, 'Abraham, Abraham!' And he said, 'Here am I.' He said, 'Do not lay your hand on the lad or do anything to him; for now I know that you fear God, seeing you have not withheld your son, your only son, from me.' And Abraham lifted up his eyes and looked, and behold, behind him was a ram, caught in a thicket by his horns; and Abraham went and took the ram, and offered it up as a burnt offering instead of his son. So Abraham called the name of the place 'The Lord will provide'; as it is said to this day, 'On the mount of the Lord it shall be provided.'

And the angel of the Lord called to Abraham a second time from heaven and said, 'By myself I have sworn, says the Lord, because you have done this, and have not withheld your son, your only son. I will indeed bless you, and I will multiply your descendants as the stars of heaven and as the sand which is on the seashore. And your descendants shall possess the gate of their enemies, and by your descendants shall all the nations of the earth bless themselves, because you have obeyed my voice.'

Genesis 22.1–18

Moslems, who constructed one of their most prestigious mosques in the site of the sacrifice, thus 'blessing' themselves 'by the name of the descendants of the patriarch'.

Who is this God who calls Abraham?

As St Augustine once observed, when God reveals himself to humanity he first manifests himself in the form of human desire: 'For the hungry he is bread, for the thirsty he is water.' But very soon God departs from human expectation because he is other. Once a person begins to go towards the response that he sees to his desire, the horizon, which seemed to be close, gets further and further away, and the adventure goes on. To attain the success to which one fundamentally aspires, one has to accept the demise of one's most immediate expectations.

Are we to suppose, then, that here God is only the mask of human desire? In that case the call heard by Abraham to sacrifice his son would not have been the expression of the will of God but the projection of a hidden desire within the patriarch himself. Might Abraham have unconsciously wished the death of his son? An apparently absurd hypothesis! Is not Isaac the 'only' son, the 'beloved' son?

But modern thought has shed some strange light at this point. The philosopher Hegel already noted that 'the birth of children is the death of parents', since every birth recalls to them in an indirect way the moment when they will have to efface themselves, carried off by the current of rising life. Descendants therefore can both give a certain feeling of the extension of the self and of survival and help parents to come to terms with death: tomorrow, the son or daughter will take the place of the father and the mother. From now on they will 'devour their lives'.

Most recent psychology has gone deep into this intuition and shown the extent to which apparently the purest sentiments can be terribly ambiguous; it has revealed the truth behind the old myth which tells how the father of Oedipus, warned of the threat that a son posed to him, tried to suppress him at birth. Among the Canaanites, at all events, the sacrifice of the firstborn son was not a myth, and it could well be explained by some obscure desire of the human heart. Those numberless abortions to get rid of the awkward child (preventing it from living its life) and those martyr children in whom the parents find a ready victim for their aggression are no longer myths. Parental love is not as directly clear and natural as one might want to believe, and it can turn into its opposite. Thus the story of Abraham might reveal a hidden face of human desire until this is found, grasped and converted by the second divine call: to let the child live.

The significance of the 'test'

Illuminating though this way of plumbing the ambiguity of the human heart may be, it still does not really take account of the text. For it is said that God *himself* sought to put Abraham to the test, and it is because the patriarch passed the test that God renewed his promise and gave Abraham his blessing. So it is impossible to dissociate this God from all responsibility in the call to sacrifice Isaac.

Is it not in fact necessary for parents (the father in a patriarchal culture) to accept the 'loss' of their child so that he may live and they may discover the real meaning of procreation?

Your children are not your children.
They are the sons and daughters of the call of life to itself,

runs a poem by the Lebanese poet Khalil Gibran.

It goes on:

> They come through you, but not of you.
> And although they are with you they do not
>   belong to you . . .
> You can try to be with them, but do not try to
>   make them as you are.
> For life does not go backwards, nor does it stop
>   with yesterday.
> You are the living bows from whom your
>   children are shot like living arrows . . .

But is not the most spontaneous feature of parental desire the desire to have the child 'for oneself'? Certainly parents want descendants. Here children no longer appear a threat but as hope and promise; however, this hope and promise can be no more than nostalgia for the past, for a life that is running out; a concern to guarantee for oneself an existence which seems to be slipping away. Do not the father and mother hope to realize vicariously, through son and daughter, all those dreams which they carry around but which, whatever their success, they have never been able to satisfy? Do they not expect to reproduce themselves, to rediscover themselves, in the new beings who will give them a satisfying and soothing image of themselves? In specific terms they will have already decided in their most secret depths that the child will be this or that. They will have determined his or her life in advance. But by thus keeping it for themselves, they prevent the child from really becoming himself or herself.

The need for a salvation

In this way we can see the ambiguity of this desire that can take the name of love. We have already discovered it behind the impulse which projects one man or woman towards another: it is equally likely to be present at the heart of parental feelings.

Once more, we see that love needs to be saved, and that it can only be saved through a 'death', a death which in reality will not be that of the son but of a certain desire. The true sacrifice is finally that of Abraham, who stops seeing his son as himself.

Then comes salvation. For God gives life to what has truly been offered to him. Isaac is restored to Abraham. However, the child who has been restored is no longer the same. He is 'other': no longer simply the object of parental desire but seen to have been given in grace (God provides) and from now on with an aura of that freedom which comes from God.

And at the same time Abraham discovers what he truly expects of his child. He himself is fully alive, the aura of the divine blessing. He too is saved. His true descendants are assured.

Much later, the Christian author of the Letter to the Hebrews could comment:

> By faith Abraham, when he was tested, offered up Isaac, and he who had received the promises was ready to offer up his only son, of whom it was said, 'Through Isaac shall your descendants be named.' He considered that God was able to raise men even from the dead; hence, figuratively speaking, he did receive him back.

Hebrews 11.17–19

From Isaac to Jesus: the revelation of the true parental relationship

In the Christian perspective Abraham always points to Jesus, the one who is the 'perfecter of faith' (Hebrews 12.1). It is Christ who unveils to the full the meaning of the old stories.

Photo Pascale L R

The story of the virginal conception and the birth of Jesus already raise in disconcerting terms the significance of a generation which is fully spiritual before being physical, and which by virtue of the fact explodes the laws of biology. For the child is engendered by the Spirit, and Joseph must accept the fact that he is not his physical father (Matthew 1.18–25). At the time of the presentation in the Temple, Mary herself must see and accept the moment when the son to whom she has given birth escapes her, piercing her heart (Luke 2.35). The sacrifice of the child is present in the first chapters of the Gospel.

But the significance of true parenthood is expressed in an even more luminous way in the episode of Jesus in the Temple:

Now his parents went to Jerusalem every year at the feast of the Passover. And when he was twelve years old, they went up according to custom, and when the feast was ended, as they were returning, the boy Jesus stayed behind in Jerusalem. His parents did not know it, but supposing him to be in the company they went a day's journey, and they sought him among their kinsfolk and acquaintances; and when they did not find him, they returned to Jerusalem, seeking him.

After three days they found him in the temple, sitting among the teachers, listening to them and asking them questions; and all who heard him were amazed at his understanding and his answers. And when they saw him they were astonished; and his mother said to him, 'Son, why have you treated us so? Behold, your father and I have been looking for you anxiously.' And he said to them, 'How is it that you sought me? Did you not know that I must be in my Father's house?' And they did not understand the saying which he spoke to them.

Luke 2.41–50

'Who is my mother? Who are my brothers?' Jesus was to ask later when his family once again went in search of him, disturbed and scandalized to see him escaping from the sacred circle of the family. And he replied, looking at the disciples around him, 'Here is my mother and here are my brothers. Whoever does the will of God is my brother and my sister and my mother' (Mark 3.33–43). The child has escaped his parents, the one called by God has broken open the closed world in which they tried to shut him up. But that is when the true family is born, in the light of the divine vocation. What appeared a break, death, becomes fertility, life.

So we are progressively led towards the saving act *par excellence*: the cross. There Mary sees her son die. She has to accept it. But through death life asserts itself once more: Jesus lives for ever and the abandoned mother becomes the mother of an immense posterity.

But why this death? What idea does it give us of the one whom Jesus called 'My Father' and whose will he claimed to be doing? That of a wrathful divine father, aggressive and vindictive, who had resolved on this tragic death to pay for the slight done to his dignity by human sin? Some Christian interpretations of the passion of Christ have taken this line. They are untenable.

Certainly the death of Jesus is the result of human sin, and 'he was pierced for our sins' (Isaiah 53.5). But by going to his death voluntarily, Jesus was simply responding with the gift of himself in total trust to the free gift of the God whose Son he claimed to be, thus bringing to its climax, in full liberty, the immeasurable communication of the love which had been his throughout his earthly existence. In this way he reveals this 'fatherhood from which every fatherhood takes its name' (Ephesians 3.14); that of a God who is the source, but who engenders only by the generous gift of himself to bring life in the freedom of free exchange.

'God did not spare his own Son, but delivered

him up for us', says St Paul (Romans 8.32). But there is no hint here of an unhealthy death-wish. God 'did not spare him' because in his love he did not relieve him of his freedom but called on him to love to the end. So he found in him the true response to this generative love. Eternally born of God, Jesus, raised up by the Spirit, made himself truly Son of the God of love by dying through love. The gift responds to the gift, grace to grace.

Human procreation under the sign of the free gift

From now on it is possible to understand all that distinguishes a certain desire for a child from the fullness of love which wants the child, consenting to the child as to a gift which comes to complete the mutual self-giving of husband and wife. The ancient theologians said that love 'diffuses itself'. Just as in his most intimate being God the Father engenders and leads on the Son, the reflection of his gift, in the movement of trinitarian love, so this same God raises up a creation that he commits in turn in the adventure of love. But to respond to its profound vocation this creation makes itself creative. 'The image of God', the human couple, brings forth offspring. It remains open to the future and it can enter into the realm of giving and receiving, of grace and of gift.

That explains the statements made by the church, which are often so misunderstood, about the place of the child within marriage. The church condemns abortion as quite contrary, not only to the biological drive, but even more to the

Family at prayer. *Photo R. Tournus*

spirituality of grace. But it also censures a whole system of human devices in which it detects all the traps of a self-centred desire which is concerned to achieve a spurious security by artifice. It questions the values of a 'balanced' marriage, of the 'blossoming of the life of the married couple', when it discovers in them a desire to avoid gift and sacrifice at any price.

Does that mean that these two latter ideals have no meaning? Certainly not. Under the pretext of generosity a kind of 'natalism', too, can sometimes mask false values, in this case a rejection of the demands involved in really bringing the child into the world, with all their biological and cultural implications; it can represent a failure to understand true responsible fatherhood or motherhood.

In this book we cannot go into the whole debate surrounding the practical morality of marriage. There are a great many books in this area. They range from the great papal encyclicals, of which *Humanae Generis* of Paul VI is the most recent to have been produced, to the great moral reminders of the *magisterium*, by way of innumerable deep studies of the problem in depth, including discussions or statements by eminent theologians of practical conclusions drawn from the basic demands of the ethics of grace. Here the 'language of principles' and 'educative language' are not always immediately in harmony, even if both tend constantly to recall the profound vocation of human love: the freedom of the gift.

'God, the Lord of life, has entrusted to men . . .'

God, the Lord of life, has entrusted to men the noble mission of safeguarding life, and men must carry it out in a manner worthy of themselves. Life must be protected with the utmost care from the moment of conception: abortion and infanticide are abominable crimes. Man's sexuality and the faculty of reproduction wondrously surpass the endowments of lower forms of life; therefore the acts proper to married life are to be ordered according to authentic human dignity and must be honoured with the greatest reverence. When it is a question of harmonizing married love with the responsible transmission of life, it is not enough to take only the good intention and the evaluation of motives into account; the objective criteria must be used, criteria drawn from the nature of the human person and human action, criteria which respect the total meaning of mutual self-giving and human procreation in the context of true love; all this is possible only if the virtue of married chastity is seriously practised. In questions of birth regulation the sons of the Church, faithful to these principles, are forbidden to use methods disapproved of by the teaching authority of the church in its interpretation of the divine law.

Vatican II, *Pastoral Constitution on the Church in the Modern World*, 51

8

How do we talk about Christian Marriage Today?

Given the problems raised by married life nowadays,
what do we say and how do we say it?

Restating the problem of marriage on the basis of the problem of faith

It is useless to want to put forward a Christian response to the difficulties and contradictions that one comes across nowadays in connection with married life unless one begins by raising the basic question of belief in Jesus Christ and in his church.

Granted, the church maintains that marriage is a human fact which it does not create. So it affirms that the demands of love belong to the *natural* order. In this sense it continues to address its message about marriage to all people of good will, whether or not they are Christians. But it also remembers that it has only truly grasped the justification behind the natural order in the light of the total revelation of love, in Jesus Christ. 'If such is the case of a man with his wife, it is not expedient to marry,' argued the disciples when they heard Jesus condemning divorce. But he replied: 'Not all men can receive this precept, but only those to whom it is given' (Matthew 19.10–11).

It is in fact impossible to raise in all their

magnitude those questions which relate to love and marriage without asking about the ultimate meaning of life.

Now it has to be noted that the teaching of the church on marriage has often lost credibility in our world because Christianity has itself lost its original character of a true brotherhood and sisterhood which proclaims by its very existence the renewal of life prompted by faith in Jesus Christ. Integrated into society, contaminated by its values, the Christian community no longer emerges as a truly alternative society, suggesting other ways of living, other values, another way of finding a place in the world. Monopolized by an individualistic liberal society, it has become simply the religious complement to an existence which too often unfolds on the basis of material and emotional interests alone. It is no more than an element of comfort and security, a guarantee against risks in the world beyond. It does not call for a total reorientation of existence. Many people would feel that such a reorientation is reserved for religious and priests, in other words those who have accepted celibacy, those who are thought to have nothing to say about love because they live in a different world. In such conditions Christian marriage appears only as one consumer article among others which

the church has to provide. (There are those who say that one has a 'right' to be married in church!) Any demands on the part of the church are seen as the price to be paid in return for this right. That is to lapse into a commercial view which gets in the way of understanding the renewal brought by the Christian vision of marriage and love.

However, a number of young people today are in search of what might be an alternative society to give meaning to their life. They hope to find a new way by means of different forms of groupings (various communities, the ecological movement . . .). The couples that they form spontaneously are often the expression of their profound need to rediscover an interpersonal communication for which they find no other possibilities around them.

Christians will only be able to offer such people a reply if they work effectively and specifically to restore the value of the fundamental sacrament: the church, a living community which inaugurates and announces the true kingdom of God. Teaching about married life is and will remain a dead letter, an ineffectual incantation, as long as it appears only as a detached element of a totality which alone offers a view of the total renewal which Jesus offered.

Explaining the significance of the moral law

Because it lives by faith and therefore perceives in the light of faith the meaning and the demands of marriage, because it has drawn conclusions from an experience lasting over millennia and to some degree finds itself an 'expert in humanity', the church is called to teach an ethical doctrine. It cannot accept moral relativism nor founder in the permissiveness that the world would want to

make universal.

'You must not eat of the fruit of the tree of the knowledge of good and evil.' The original prohibition reported in the book of Genesis recalls that man is not master of the law, that he has nothing freely. It indicates the necessary limit of the human dream: the creature does not remake creation. Man, born of this nature, is called on to

Guillaume de Vandemont returning from a crusade, greeted by his wife Nancy. Chapelle des Cordeliers. *Arch. Photo Paris*

humanize it. But in order for that to happen he has to respect it, it and its immanent rules.

Beyond question the appeal to nature is sometimes ambiguous. Facts which were in reality no more than relative cultural traditions, if not the prejudices of social groups, have too easily been declared 'natural', and therefore absolute. The clearest example of this is the idea of the 'weaker sex' and the strong sex: this is a generalization at a psychological and social level of a straightforward physiological difference in behaviour and reactions. In fact human beings never exist in the natural state but are always moulded by the society in which they are immersed. So there is a danger of wanting to reject *a priori* any development of the idea that one gets of human possibilities. We know that love has not been lived out in the same way at all times and in all civilizations.

By virtue of its reflection and experience extending over time, the Christian community notes that the authentic realization of married life follows a certain trajectory and that it carries with it the recognition of rules of conduct. All our biblical reflection has shown us how these came gradually to be recognized.

Thus, in his encounter with the other in love, man has to admit that his actions are not a matter of indifference. There are those which sterilize and kill and those which make life. One can try to close one's eyes to these facts, but they cannot be suppressed. The law is a simple reminder of this harsh truth. Those who cannot face it will never be truly free.

One can certainly regret that the form sometimes given to this doctrine prevents people from seeing the educational concern which ought always to be present behind a reminder of the law. One might also think that a deeper reflection on the true demands of nature is necessary. But the church would fail in its vocation if it gave up saying, 'You must' or 'You must not', even if it entails explaining again, each time, the reason why this is so.

'If you love me, keep my commandments,' said Jesus (John 14.15). These commandments are not arbitrary. They are the expression of the logic of law. They are no less commandments, marking out the true way that men and women are called on to take. And no Christian can allow them deliberately to be hidden or forgotten.

These are 'natural' laws which the church rediscovers in the significance of the creation as affirmed by the Bible. It reminds Christians of them, stressing that faith gives them grace to see more intensely the profound significance of love: all love comes from God and leads to God. For God is himself Love and humanity finds its ultimate worth in the fact that it has been created in the image of God and is capable of love as he is.

Adopting an attitude of counselling

Recalling basic principles and the law is not the only language which Christians use. Aware of the courses that men and woman in fact follow, they know the need to accompany their brothers and sisters along the roads which lead to maturity. Reminding themselves of the history of the people of God (and of what was and still is their journey towards the full comprehension of love), they understand the need for an attitude of counselling: one which will help others to go forward from the point where they are. That is certainly true of priests responsible for marriage preparation, but it is also and indeed all the more true for parents, marriage counsellors, teachers and friends consulted in confidence.

It is certainly easy to proclaim an ideal and to describe what ought to be an impeccable way of arriving with certainty at the envisaged destination. The call for the perfection of a love marked by respect and generosity, one day ending up in true and total encounter with the other person, describes a splendid road to take. But the real history of individuals and groups is always made up of histories. The concrete reality of human beings consists in accidents and failings. An authentic sexual relationship can only be discovered by difficult searching, if not mistakes, not to mention sin. Often a recognition of the right road only comes after the exploration of certain spiritual, emotional and physical dead ends.

The language of counselling takes account of these detours. It does not judge, but offers help on the journey towards the end in view. It believes that faults, unfortunate adventures, failure, can also lead to new beginnings. The counsellor is aware of the risks. But he knows that these have to be accepted, because they are a condition of growth. He does not dramatize a failure, but does everything possible to make it the occasion for a new beginning. He goes along with those who walk in the night, remembering his own darkness, so that little by little the light may appear.

This language of counselling is that of the Bible. It can only fail to be understood by those who, in search of an absolute security, refuse to make any journey at all and wrap themselves up in the law, forgetting their own weakness. So Jesus made mortal enemies of those to whom he dared to say, 'Let him who is without sin among you cast the first stone.' It is the same today: anyone who wants to help a brother or sister in difficulty must try to welcome and understand him or her, even if that brings down hosility and criticism from those who are established in their false certainties.

Parents, priests, educators are here thrown back on themselves, on their capacity to affirm truly that by which they live, that in which they believe, on their capacity to understand and discover that they themselves cannot claim to say the last word on the way in which one can live out a sexual relationship. They may be led to accept situations which go against their own profound convictions. They may also truly rediscover the profound significance of marriage as a result of contact with these situations. The essential thing is that real communication can continue to operate between all those who at the same time find themselves challenged by the profound reality of Love. Then history will go forward and the future will remain open.

Some 'laws' of marriage recalled by the Second Vatican Council

In the Pastoral Constitution on The Church in the Modern World (*Gaudium et Spes*), Vatican II states:

The intimate partnership of life and the love which constitutes the married state has been established by the creator and endowed by him with its own proper laws: it is rooted in the contract of its partners, that is, in their irrevocable personal consent. It is an institution confirmed by the divine law and receiving its stability, even in the eyes of society, from the human act by which the partners mutually surrender themselves to each other; for the good of the partners, of the children, and of society this sacred bond no longer depends on human decision alone. For God himself is the author of marriage . . . By its very nature the institution of marriage and married love is ordered to the procreation and education of the offspring and it is in them that it finds its crowning glory. Thus the man and woman, who 'are no longer two but one' (Matthew 19.6), help and serve each other by their marriage partnership; they become conscious of their unity and experience it more deeply from day to day. The intimate union of marriage, as a mutual giving of two persons, and the good of the children demand total fidelity from the spouses and require an unbreakable unity between them (48.1).

. . . The acts in marriage by which the intimate and chaste union of the spouses takes place are noble and honourable; the truly human performance of these acts fosters the self-giving they signify and enriches the spouses in joy and gratitude. Endorsed by mutual fidelity and, above all, consecrated by Christ's sacrament, this love abides faithfully in mind and body in prosperity and adversity and hence excludes both adultery and divorce. The unity of marriage, distinctly recognized by our Lord, is made clear in the equal personal dignity which must be accorded to man and wife in mutual and unreserved affection (49.2).

Conclusion

All through these pages I have tried to show what significance Christian marriage can have at a time when it is no longer self-evident, when it is no longer imposed by a Christian society but has increasingly become a matter for free choice.

So it is impossible to give a quick answer to the question, 'Must one get married in church?' At most one can say, 'Yes, if you believe in Jesus Christ, if you have a deep understanding of the meaning of love, if you accept the call which the church makes to live marriage in fullness and truth, if you expect spiritual support from it, if you expect God's help.'

But it is, on the other hand, possible to ask the question in another way: when must one get married in church?

The answer is one which applies in the case of all the sacraments: when those who ask for marriage believe in what the church offers them; when they come to ask God in trust to ratify their love and to help them to live it out in fullness.

There is no need for everything to be quite clear: faith is not manifest clarity, but the perception of a clarity which shines in the night and which allows one to take bearings by it.

There is no need to 'be sure'. Nothing is more dangerous than a claim to certainty which is not in fact based on more than an essentially transitory sentiment. What is infinitely more sure is the humility of those who are aware of the difficulties, who recognize that they themselves are frail and therefore call on God as he is known in Jesus Christ. Only the penumbra of this God can be seen. Again, love itself offers a better vision of God as the infinite Love in whom we trust. This is where the gospel saying, 'Lord I believe, help thou my unbelief', holds true.

For certain young Christians, this marriage in church will be the real beginning of their married life and that is what the church desires to be the norm for true believers. For others, it will come only at the end of a slow process of discovery which includes the experience of living together. No one has the role of deciding the time when God himself will give the sign and invite those in love to come and share in his vintage feast. But all are invited, and the last will have just as good a place as the first (see the Parable of the Workers at the Eleventh Hour in Matthew 20.1–16).

Sooner or later, the moment will come when Christian marriage will regain its true significance. Far from being a pure formality, it will constitute a response to the call of God to love as he has taught us to love through his Son.

What about trial marriages?

This formula became very popular for a number of years though it is now used less, and rightly so. It is a contradiction in terms.

The notion of marriage presupposes total commitment, a gift without second thoughts. It includes duration, fidelity. So it does not lend itself to experimentation. To say 'we are together for life' implies a quest for the other partner, an attention to his or her own personality which does not *a priori* call for living together to 'see how it goes'.

Unquestionably, certain 'experiences' go beyond this stage and profoundly involve the participants. In that case we have the rejection of an institution, but not of the reality of marriage.

In this sphere, as in many others, one has to mistrust ready-made formulae.

F. Monfort

'An even greater mystery . . .'

Here is an even greater mystery: no one comes to know himself or herself through introspection, or in the solitude of a personal diary. Rather, it is in dialogue, in meeting other persons. It is only by expressing one's convictions to others that one becomes really conscious of them. Anyone who wants to see himself or herself clearly must open up to a confidant freely chosen and worthy of such trust. It may be a friend just as easily as a doctor; it may also be one's marital partner.

Marriage then becomes a great adventure, a continuous discovery both of oneself and of one's mate. It becomes a daily broadening of one's horizon, an opportunity of learning something new about life, about human existence, about God. This is why in the beginning of the Bible God says, 'It is not good that man should be alone.' Man here means the human being: 'It is not good that the human being should be alone.' The human being needs fellowship; he or she needs a partner, a real encounter with others; needs to understand others and to feel understood by them.

Paul Tournier, *Marriage Difficulties*, SCM Press and John Knox Press 1967
(US title *To Understand Each Other*)

Declaration of nullity

While the church does not accept divorce, it does recognize that there are cases in which a marriage is null: certain conditions essential to matrimonial commitment are lacking. If this deficiency can be proved, the church, through the intermediary of competent tribunals, recognizes the nullity of the marriage. The marriage is not broken: it is said not really to have taken place.

Each diocese has its own tribunal, to which anyone should go in cases where they have serious reasons for supposing that a matrimonial commitment has not been seriously entered into.

The ecclesiastical tribunal in Rome is a body charged with judging in the last instances cases

→

which it has not been possible to settle at the level of the local church. So it is a mistake to think that declarations on the nullity of marriage necessarily come from Rome.

Like any procedure which involves work, a declaration of nullity of marriage costs money.

But so that the question of money does not hinder the introduction of a case, the church always offers the possibility of itself becoming responsible for expenses arising out of the examination of a marriage where the parties concerned do not have adequate resources.

Beyond death

Given the Christian significance of marital fidelity, the husband or wife of a spouse snatched away by death cannot but raise the question of fidelity beyond death.

This fidelity should not be turned backwards on a vanished past in a barren way. That is why the church has always recognized the right of remarriage. St Paul already advised young widows who could not bear their difficult condition to take a new spouse. This is not a matter of destroying an authentic love so much as reviving it by making a new home. There are remarriages which are authentic forms of continuity, which do not forget the partner who has passed away but are concerned to renew the experience of life with him or her.

But Paul also rejoiced to see certain widows

ready to turn totally to the Lord (I Corinthians 7.8).

I Timothy gives some indication of the requirements for membership of what seems to have formed a particular group, with very precise functions, in the primitive church: widows, bound by a true commitment, must not be less than sixty, must have been married only once, and must have a good reputation (5.3–16).

The renewed recognition of the way in which marriage can lead to holiness should have led to further reflection on this problem. At present in the church there is a revival of groups of those who have been widowed (particularly widows), the distinctive character of which is recognized by the church.

The remarriage of divorced people

The Christian ideal of marriage envisages a married couple living together in fidelity. All Christian churches agree on this principle: total love is irreversible, and anyone who wants to respond perfectly to the divine call must never despair of the other, no matter what happens. But the failure of certain marriages is a fact, and it has to be recognized that in numerous cases

life together becomes impossible, sometimes beyond doubt through the fault of one or other partner, but sometimes also as a result of circumstances in which it is impossible to speak of guilt. The decision to maintain the marriage tie in all circumstances, against all the odds, despite perhaps an inevitable separation, often presupposes a supreme degree of heroism. The church

93

can call believers to that. But how can it fail to understand some remarriages? In which case, how is it to regard them?

In practice, different churches have adopted different positions.

While not wanting to justify divorce, the Orthodox churches refuse to impose a state of perpetual celibacy on an innocent spouse betrayed by his or her partner. It allows remarriage.

In most of the Reformation churches there is a rejection of utter intransigence: this would be to forget that in Jesus Christ God forgives men and women their sin and allows them to make a new start after a failure. So the church can allow its prayers to go with a new marriage when this is the sign of a truly spiritual new beginning. On the way to the kingdom which is not yet fully present, account must be taken of human weakness, and certain deficiencies must be accepted once there is a concern to continue the way towards God.

By contrast, after many hesitations, the Roman Catholic church has firmly rejected any marriage of divorced persons. This is a consequence of its affirmation of the sacramental character of a valid marital union. Any remarriage is held to be contrary to Christian morality. Christians who infringe the law are not excommunicated, but are excluded from the sacramental life of the church (penitential absolution and eucharistic communion). But what pastor would endorse as they stand declarations like that of Leo XIII who saw remarriage as an 'abominable concubinage', or ancient canon law which spoke in this connection of 'bigamy'? The attitude of rejection has given place to an attitude of welcome and appeal: the remarriage of divorced persons does not entail total exclusion from the church nor does it definitively cut off those involved from all Christian life. We can see the progressive development of a real 'pastorate of remarried divorced persons', aimed at supporting in their faith and their spiritual life those who find themselves still excluded from complete participation in the sacraments.

Do we need to go further and cease to refuse the sacraments in all circumstances to those who, by virtue of their painful and difficult situation, perhaps need even more than others signs of the divine mercy? Some pastors think so, and in some circumstances and with certain reservations intended to preserve principles, draw practical conclusions from their view. The Roman authorities for their part reject anything which might seem to put in question the basic principle that they find it more necessary than ever to defend. At most the new Code of Canon Law authorizes more flexibility in the recognition that certain unions cannot have been contracted in conditions which allow the church to see in them the true sacramental marriage that it offers.

Is a development possible in this sphere? The way in which in the past, when faced with new problems, the church has not hesitated to adopt hitherto unprecedented attitudes, makes it necessary to guard against declarations that are too absolute. We are far from the time when the authorities condemned a murderer, a penitent apostate or an adulterer to lifelong penitence. It is surely not a matter of supposing that one could simply go from the red light to the green light, thus putting in question the very significance of Christian marriage. But legal discipline has never stopped adapting to the needs which produce a pastoral practice the ultimate motivation of which is always a concern to proclaim the good news of the faithful mercy of God in one way or another. Our biblical meditation on the course taken by God to bring men and women to discover the fullness of love compels us to remember that detours through failure or even faults can be the occasion for a new start to the divine quest. Even in the framework of the contemporary discipline of the Roman Catholic church, that is a truth which must always inspire the life of faith, hope and love among divorced persons who have remarried.

'More to understand than to be understood . . .'

You well know that beautiful prayer of Francis of Assisi: 'Lord! Grant that I may seek more to understand than to be understood . . .' It is this new desire which the Holy Spirit awakens in couples and which transforms their marriage. As long as a man is preoccupied primarily with being understood by his wife, he is miserable, overcome with self pity, the spirit of demanding, and bitter withdrawal. As soon as he becomes preoccupied with understanding her, seeking to understand that which he had not before understood, and with his own wrongdoing in not having understood her, then the direction taken by events begins to change. You know those films in which the automobile wheels seem to turn backward because of the timing of the film's frames, unseen by our eyes. Well, this same type of wheel, this same chain of events which drives the person who feels misunderstood to withdraw into himself, and thus to be ever less understood, this vicious circle can be reversed when it is seen in a new light. As soon as a person feels understood, he or she opens up, and by lowering his or her defences is also able to be better understood.

Paul Tournier, *Marriage Difficulties*

Beyond the mist, second love

Marriage is not only the fulfillment of the immediate love which brings a man and woman together, it is also the slow transfiguration of that love through the experiences of common reality. Early love does not yet see this reality, for the pull of the heart and senses bewitches it. Only gradually does reality establish itself, when eyes have been opened to the shortcomings and failures revealed by everyday life. He who can accept the other then, as he really is, in spite of all disappointments, who can share the joys and plagues of daily life with him just as he has shared the great experience of early love, who can walk with him before God and with God's strength, will achieve second love, the real mystery of marriage. This is as far superior to first love as the mature person is to the child, as the self-conquering heart is to that which simply allows itself to be conquered. At the cost of much sacrifice and effort something great has come into being. Strength, profound loyalty, and a stout heart are necessary to avoid the illusions of passion, cowardice, selfishness and violence.

R. Guardini, *The Lord*, Longmans 1956

No holding back

There are very religious people who remain distant and hidden and who are considered indifferent by their partner or their pastor. There are also couples who can pray together without really expressing to one another their ideas on the questions that faith poses for them. There is thus need for bringing faith and life together, if faith is to make a difference and if life is to be transformed. A bringing together of faith and marital life is needed, so that faith may bring its incomparable transforming power and its understanding, and so that marital life may attain its fullness.

How can the two be brought together? That depends less upon what we do than upon what we are. It is more a matter of attitude than of method. We can at any rate ask God to lead us there, to show us the way, himself to bring about this total unity which is, according to his plan, to be the experience of marriage.

Whatever one's past experiences may have been, new clouds will always appear. Just as soon, then, as our sensitive feelings are again hurt, our first instinctive reaction will always be to clam up, to withdraw, and to hide our real self. But in our silent moments in God's presence, silent moments so full of truth, love, and respect for others, a second movement of the soul can bring us to overcome this holding back of ourselves which took over so quickly and which could again jeopardize our marital oneness. Because of such moments we have come to experience much more than a wonderful marriage; we have come, through each other, to experience God himself.

Paul Tournier, *Marriage Difficulties*

'Through her I know that I am alive'

A leper-house . . . In the most distressing, odious sense of the term . . . People doing nothing, for whom nothing can be done, going round and round in their courtyard, in their cage.

People alone; worse – abandoned. For whom everything is already silence and night.

But one of them – just one – has kept clear eyes. He can smile, and say 'Thank you' when someone offers him something.

One of them – just one – has remained human.

The nun wanted to know the reason for this miracle. What kept him alive . . . She watched him.

And she saw how every day, above that high, harsh wall, a face appeared. Just the tip of a woman's face, about the size of a fist, smiling. The man was there, waiting to get this smile, the food for his strength and hope . . . He smiled back and the face disappeared. Then he began again on his wait until the next day.

When the missionary surprised them, he said, simply, 'It's my wife.'

And after a silence: 'Before I came here she looked after me secretly. With everything that she could find. A fetishist had given her a ointment. She anointed my face with it every day . . . except for a little corner. Just enough to put her lips there . . . But it was no good. Then they caught me. But she followed me. And when I see her every day, through her I know that I am alive . . .'

R. Follereau, *Pour toi mon amour*, Cerf 1981